LIGHTING
THE WAY

LIGHTING THE WAY

Stories that Show How Our Culture Went Wrong and How We Can Restore Order

By John Horvat II and Norman J. Fulkerson

The American Society for the Defense of Tradition, Family, and Property—TFP

© Copyright 2018 The American Society for
the Defense of Tradition, Family, and Property®—TFP®
For information about special discounts for bulk sales, please contact:
Return to Order
P.O. Box 1337, Hanover, PA 17331
Tel.: (885) 861-8420
Email: Info@returntoorder.org

Several chapters of this book were taken from the following articles by John
Horvat II that were reprinted and adapted with permission of *Crisis Magazine*:
• Advice to Graduating Millennials: Don't Jump the Ropes
• Rediscovering the Ideal Healthcare Plan
• The Strong Money of Saint Louis
• Where are the Nation's Captains?
• How Material Things Can Lead Us to God

Grateful acknowledgment is made to the Intercollegiate Studies Institute for
permission to publish: Culture is in the Grits by John Horvat II

ISBN: 9781877905537
Library of Congress Control Number: 2018939607

Printed in the United States of America

TABLE OF CONTENTS

PART III

A Passion for Justice

PART IV

Representative Characters

PART V

When Men Dream

My *Return to Order* Moments

I do not remember when the expression was coined, but it started to appear a bit after the book, *Return to Order*, was published. I would find myself in situations where I could observe examples in daily life of the book's theoretical principles. When I would describe these incidents to others, people very naturally started calling them "*Return to Order* moments."

Return to Order moments are not events that you can plan. In a very organic manner, they just happen. When you least expect it, a principle of the book jumps out at you. These incidents can be negative or positive. Sometimes, they deal with the frustrations of our hectic high-tech world. Other times, these moments might involve relationships, skills, or conversations. They need not be events, since they can happen with a sudden insight gained by reading a newspaper article or book. At other times, they involve a touching display of veneration and respect for traditional values.

For those not familiar with the book, *Return to Order: From a Frenzied Economy to an Organic Christian Society—Where We've Been, How We Got Here, and Where We Need to Go,* let me explain what the book contains. It deals with the present frenzied society and its effect on our lives and culture. As a solution, the book proposes an organic Christian society which is made up of those natural regulating institutions of family, community, and Faith that keep a society in balance. For this reason, there is a broad range of topics—good and bad—that can serve as occasions for *Return to Order* moments to happen.

An Example of One Moment

One of the first such moments happened when some friends and I were visiting Charleston, South Carolina, while promoting the book in that lovely city. As any good visitor to the city should do, we took advantage of our stay to stroll around the historic downtown and admire its many beautiful antebellum houses and cobblestone streets.

The old city is almost a living exhibit of organic society described in

Return to Order. The design, color, and decoration of each house display the vivid personality of the families that built them. Many of them played some role in the history of the city, the state, or in some cases, the nation. Some houses are still owned by the descendants of the original builder. I was enthralled.

We stopped for lunch at Poogan's Porch, one of the city's excellent restaurants. This particular place had originally been a Civil War–era house and was very well preserved. As we were conversing over plates of traditional South Carolina low country cuisine, two ladies in full Victorian dress entered the room and sat down.

We were convinced that they were local ladies working as tour guides for one of the many house museums. One lady seemed to confirm this impression by answering her iPhone at the table in a very un-Victorian manner. I commented with my friends about the contradiction between her dress and the iPhone.

Then the *Return to Order* moment happened.

A Sudden Change

Apparently, the lady overheard my commentary and after finishing her call came over to the table and introduced herself. She then apologized for being on the phone in her Victorian dress. As if to re-establish her credibility, she explained that there was a pressing matter at home that forced her to answer the phone.

As it turns out, they were not tour guides or even locals, but members of a Victorian society visiting from Minnesota. As part of their efforts to preserve nineteenth century culture, they were touring Charleston dressed in authentic Victorian clothing. These ladies were the real thing who went beyond the externals and desired to value and live the principles of that era.

As we spoke, others started to listen in—these restaurants are all very cozy places. Someone at our table asked for a picture to remember the moment.

The flash set off something almost more interesting than the ladies themselves. Soon, other people in the restaurant were asking for pictures. Men and women in shorts, untucked T-shirts, and flip-flops were enchanted with the two ladies and lined up to take pictures with them.

The experience got me thinking: As mentioned in *Return to Order*, many people are looking beyond the frenetic intemperance of modern life and have longings for order and authenticity. The incident at Poogan's showed me that, much more than we realize, Americans—and, surprisingly, young Americans—have an attraction and admiration for traditional culture, customs, ways of dress, traditional food, and regional cuisine and architecture. The incident was a touching confirmation of passages from *Return to Order*.

The Birth of a Book

Later I was commenting with my good friend Norman Fulkerson that such moments are much more common than we realize. In fact, I have long admired the fascinating articles he has written over the course of his travels on what I do not hesitate to call "*Return to Order* moments."

Mr. Fulkerson and I were both personally formed in the school of the Brazilian Catholic thinker Prof. Plinio Corrêa de Oliveira that emphasizes this more cultural approach to the analysis of reality. It was not long before we agreed to work together on a collection of essays and stories of these special moments.

Like *Return to Order*, this book is a project of the American Society for the Defense of Tradition, Family, and Property (TFP), of which we are both members. Our goal in writing this book is to prove that *Return to Order* is not just a theoretical work, but something that is lived daily in America. It is to be found everywhere, especially when you least expect it.

This is a hidden America that is often ignored by the media. Indeed, many would prefer not to acknowledge the existence of this America that so contradicts the worn-out narrative of an always progressing nation evolving toward new levels of materialistic, secular enlightenment.

At the same time, this is not your typical "finding the real America" book of quaint little stories and observations of dying America traditions.

A Polarized America

Ours are tales of a polarized nation at a crossroads. Thus, you will see examples and stories of the good and the bad, the best and worst of what is presently happening across the country. We have also included a few examples of cases outside the country as models of what we do or do not want. We will bring you absurd stories that will make you shake your head in disbelief, and others that will fill you with wonder and joy.

The first section will deal with the effects of throwing off restraint.

We will see cases of what I call the frenetic intemperance of our times. We can see this frenetic intemperance in the frenzied desires of people who want everything now—instantly and effortlessly. All too often, it leads to people treating others like numbers and machines. Everything becomes standardized and soulless. Individualism and materialism dominate in this kind of society, and often lead us on a frustrated quest for perfect happiness and unbridled freedom. All this has its negative effect upon us and the culture. It is self-destructive and, if unopposed, will eventually lead to our ruin. Our treatment of this negative theme will be limited, however, since it makes no sense to dwell upon a present that has no future.

Hope for America's Future

The remaining parts of this book are much longer and deal with the more positive aspects of American reality. They address what I call organic solutions inside the context of an organic Christian society.

The best thing about organic solutions is that they are not theoretical plans or government programs that claim to fix everything. They naturally appear, much like my *Return to Order* moments, when you least expect them, and especially when there is the right mix of virtue, ingenuity, and occasion. These moments can be found in experiences, news items, or readings.

What Mr. Fulkerson and I do is demonstrate that these solutions are happening now. They are all around us if we only take notice. There is hope for America. These solutions can be found and are being found—and Americans love them.

Where to Look for Solutions

America's future can be found in the excellence of the "Ham Lady" of Princeton, Kentucky, the meticulous work of a local jeweler, or the American cheese artisans that rival their French counterparts.

Across the nation, we find those looking for authenticity and order. Whether it be organic food, Gregorian chant, a desire for craftsmanship, the traditional family, homeschooling, or microbreweries, there is a groundswell of those who want something different from the frenetic intemperance of our days. There are sizeable minorities out there who react with great passion and courage. They dare to defy the culture and say "enough."

Our stories will also deal with the key role of individuals and families in making organic solutions happen. We will look at what I call "representative characters," those people, like Shirley the shuttle driver, who step up to the plate and take upon themselves responsibilities that change society.

Above all, we will give examples of the power and attraction of our Christian ideals, which are so perfectly suited to our human nature. These are marvelous and wonderful tales that represent a world in which the good, the true, and the beautiful are full of meaning. This attraction ultimately leads to God, since any return to order is also a return to God.

As the culture worsens, more and more Americans are soul-searching. They are looking for an order that they sense once existed and might yet return. Our goal is to awaken these yearnings in souls by proving this return is not only necessary, but possible.

I believe that such moments can be found everywhere. That is why I ask for and welcome the stories of readers, since each story is an impressive confirmation that a return to order is indeed part of America's future. I invite you to join this future.

You can write to John Horvat at jh1908@aol.com.

PART I

FRENETIC INTEMPERANCE: THROWING OFF RESTRAINT

In *Return to Order*, I coined the term "frenetic intemperance" to describe the root cause of what has gone wrong in our economy and culture. I explain how a lack of restraint and balance has entered all sectors of our society. Above all, I wanted to show that this is a moral problem, not an economic one.

Frenetic intemperance can be defined as a reckless and restless spirit inside some sectors of modern economy and culture that leads us to throw off legitimate restraints and gratify all desires. Each person is encouraged to live without limits or restrictions.

People come to resent the very idea of restraint and scorn the spiritual, religious, moral, and cultural values that serve to order and temper economic activity.

Frenetic intemperance is also a historic process that became dominant with the rise of the Industrial Revolution. It later created the conditions for our mass culture. It takes away that warm, human element so essential to society. Without the anchors of tradition, family, and faith, people are easily influenced by the mass media, mass markets, and lifestyles that shape their lives.

Thus, frenetic intemperance creates an economy and a society that is frenzied and out of balance. It tends to make society function like a gigantic machine in which everyone is treated the same. It leads to the standardization of things and the limiting of real choices. We can also see frenetic intemperance in the abuse of technology and social media that absorb, yet do not enrich our lives.

In this section, we present stories and news items that focus on this throwing off of all restraint and its tragic consequences. We also see what happens when extreme individualism takes hold, and people demand unbridled freedom with no rules. We look at the bland, expressionless world created by frenetic intemperance. We discuss the abuse of technology, which should serve us, but now puts us at its service.

A Whatever-Whenever-Wherever Economy

BY JOHN HORVAT II

A good definition of frenetic intemperance is found in this news article that tells the story of someone who understood the concept correctly. This father did not see frenetic intemperance as a danger, however, but as something desirable for his children. Such a desire is precisely what we and children do not need as we face life's vicissitudes. It is a recipe for disaster.

When people ask me what is wrong with our modern day economy, I respond that it is frenzied and out of balance. I explain how I coined the term "frenetic intemperance" to describe a restless and reckless spirit inside our modern economy that foments a drive to throw off legitimate restraints and gratify disordered passions. This frenetic intemperance, I explain, is where we went wrong.

The problem is that frenetic intemperance is an abstract concept. It is not immediately apparent to people as to what I mean. Thus, I am always on the lookout for examples or expressions that help to clarify the concept and make it more understandable to the man in the street.

I recently found such an example that goes a long way in explaining frenetic intemperance. It involved an article that described television-viewing habits. It said that the average American adult spends 4 hours, 31 minutes watching television each day. That might seem like a lot of viewing, but it only tells half the story.

The television screen represents yesterday's entertainment. People today also look at other screens and monitors, and so, the article notes, in addition to television viewing time, the average American adult spends yet another 5 hours, 16 minutes looking at other computer and phone screens each day.

The total of 9 hours, 47 minutes is an impressive amount of time on any screen. It indicates a certain lack of restraint that is characteristic of frenetic intemperance. There are missing priorities in these habits where the person gives in to the temptation to be constantly checking his devices. This kind of obsessive behavior is an example of what is meant by frenetic intemperance.

However, the article ended with an even more dramatic expression. It told the story of a man with three very young children who were fully hooked up to their screens. Two of the three could not even read, yet they all had Wi-Fi enabled mobile devices and could stream videos to them.

The father gloried in the fact that, "They expect to be able to see whatever they want, whenever they want, wherever they want."

Eureka! This is a perfect expression to describe frenetic intemperance. It is an economy that throws off restraint and encourages a regime in which you seek out whatever you want, whenever you can, and wherever you are.

When you apply this whatever-whenever-wherever mentality to economy, it becomes frenzied and out of balance. It leads to people wanting everything now, regardless of the consequences. Lack of resources is no obstacle for this mentality. If what you want cannot be obtained immediately, there are always credit options to make it happen now. If that does not work, there is always big government to turn things once considered privileges or luxuries into entitlements.

When society is not virtuous, a whatever-whenever-wherever mentality leads to an economy that is run by the disordered whims and passions. Reason is no longer in control, and consequently, markets are unstable and subject to crashes. Self-interest and gratification come to rule in accordance with personal preferences.

Such a conception of life calls to mind the ideas of Scottish philosopher David Hume (1711–1776) who famously wrote, "Reason is, and ought only to be the slave of the passions, and can never pretend to any other office than to serve and obey them."

The problem is that the passions can be true tyrants that do not respect reality. Real economy should be run by reason and temperance that leads men to virtue. This requires restraint, foresight, and effort. It does not exclude the orderly passions and preferences that are part of the lives of men; however, these very human and necessary elements are secondary and cannot dominate.

Our problem today is our whatever-whenever-wherever economy is taking us to our ruin. It is filling us with frenetic intemperance. What we need is a return to order.

Ten Varieties of Wheat Thins: Is There Real Choice?

BY JOHN HORVAT II

Frenetic intemperance is often manifested by a consumer paradise with a seemingly infinite number of choices. At the same time, it is also manifested by mass standardization. The two concepts appear to be contradictory. This story looks at this contradiction and exposes the poverty of choices that frenetic intemperance actually offers.

When reading the manuscript of the book *Return to Order*, one of the reviewing editors remarked that while he agreed with the book's criticism of standardization, there are still plenty of choices out there. After all, he quipped, how could he give up the ten varieties of Wheat Thins found at the local Wal-Mart?

The comment made me pause. I had to admit that he had a point. There certainly are a lot of choices out there—and yet no one can deny that there is also a lot of standardization. How do you reconcile the two things?

To solve the problem, I decided to take a trip to Wal-Mart. I just had to see these Wheat Thins for myself.

What I found was disconcerting. As you enter Wal-Mart, you are hit by row upon row of choices of just about everything. The place was huge, and it took some time to navigate my way to the Wheat Thins. Finally, I found them. There was a whole section dedicated to the snack. I found not ten varieties, but twenty-six different kinds of Wheat Thins offered in regular and exotic flavors. As I went down the aisle, there were similar findings: eighteen different types of saltines, twelve types of ginger snaps, and so on. My standardization claim was thoroughly discredited by the undeniable evidence.

Or so it seemed. There was something fishy about all this variety. I returned to the Wheat Thins and looked over the selections. Then it hit me. These Wheat Thins were all made by the same company: Nabisco. All this variety was essentially the same Wheat Thin, but with different flavorings mixed in. There were also different sizes, packaging, and colors that added to the overwhelming impression of variety. However, the long and short of it is that, as far as Wheat Thins are concerned, mighty Wal-Mart pretty much limits me to one standardized Wheat Thin with my choice of natural and artificial flavorings—likewise standardized.

The vast variety that had so impressed my editor was also standardized in time and place. This basic Wheat Thin and its flavor selections are exactly the same in the thousands of Wal-Marts and other supermarkets nationwide. The fact that I live in Pennsylvania and the editor lives in Virginia makes no difference. Moreover, I can expect the present standard wheat thin to be pretty much as it was in the past, and that it will probably be much the same in the future.

As I looked down the aisles of Wal-Mart, I saw that most products—be it yogurt or corn chips—were similarly organized. Each category is dominated by one or several giant companies, which produces a standardized basic product with a variety of standardized flavorings, packaging, and sizes.

The book *Return to Order* addresses this standardization and imagines a more organic order where the human element returns to the markets. Imagine, for example, an array of bakers making their own distinctive kind of Wheat Thins, differing from place to place with flavors based on the cultural tastes of the locale—and at competitive prices.

Who can deny that in such a society, there would be much more variety spread about the nation? There would also be much richer

choices reflecting that human element that would make the lowly Wheat Thins much more tasty and unique. It would be an expression of the culture of the people and not the frenetic intemperance of standardized mass production.

Modern supermarkets create the illusion of variety.

CHAPTER 3

Where Have All the Apples Gone?

BY JOHN HORVAT II

Those who promote frenetic intemperance like to claim that our modern economy has improved lives and choices. While life has improved through modern production techniques and scientific advances, there are other fields in which the quality of life has declined. One of these fields is the suppression of local varieties of goods and foods that are the spice of life. In this article, we will look at what was lost, using the example of apple production.

One of the benefits of modern mass markets is supposed to be the proliferation of choices. The modern consumer can choose from so many things available on a variety of platforms, be it online or off. This ability to select from plenty is considered one of the marvels of modern economy.

However, there is another side to the matter that is not often explored. In their drive to provide abundance, mass markets suppress variety. When providing many choices, they tend to offer the same universal options everywhere. Far from enriching a culture, mass markets can impoverish it.

Such a thesis might appear heretical to those who defend classic economic theory that affirms modern markets supply anything, anytime, and anywhere. Such defenders would claim this availability represents an explosion, not an implosion, of culture.

Hard to Prove the Contrary

What complicates this debate is the preconception that pre-industrial markets found in Christian civilization were so limited. The overpowering efficiency of mass markets indicts both Christian civilization and pre-industrial society. Those who criticize modern markets are often forced into silence in the face of the overwhelming evidence of how modern production and distribution networks supply our needs.

Then, suddenly, a straightforward and refreshing example appears that proves the contrary: Pre-industrial markets were not limited at all. In fact, they were incredibly rich.

The Apple: An Expressive Example

One very expressive example is that of the simple apple.

Apples have been bought and sold from time immemorial. By looking at how they are sold in pre-modern times and now, we can make a judgment on the matter.

As it stands now, we can buy apples anywhere during any season. In the off-season, apples can be shipped in from other parts of the world. Cold storage techniques extend the life of the apple for a good amount of time.

Modern Apples

Thus far, we can say modern apple markets do make apples available longer to a greater number of Americans all the time. However, the matter becomes more difficult when we look at exactly what is available to us.

The first thing that is notable is that most apples in America are not local apples. A full two-thirds of all apples are harvested in Washington State.

The second observation is that the varieties of apples available are very limited. In fact, some 90 percent of the market is made up of only fifteen types. Of those, the Red Delicious apple occupies the top position. These choices are predetermined by producers who adjust them according to their needs of production, shipping, and storage.

Thus, while the availability of apples is great in industrial society,

© Kesorriphoto | Dreamstime.com

the variety is depressingly poor. Most people are given these same choices nationwide with rarely a local apple in sight.

Pre-industrial Apples

The comparison must then be made based on what the pre-industrial apple market looked like. The first fact is that apples were grown all over the country, with each region specializing in the apples that grew best in the area.

A recent *New York Times* article reports the second astonishing fact that some 17,000 varieties of apples were grown in North America over the past few centuries.

There was an enormous variety, a wonder-world of apples, to suit every need and taste. While not everyone had access to all 17,000 varieties, no two regions experienced the same fifteen modern choices. The choices were determined by those who lived in the locality. We can say that apple selection enriched the area and the culture.

Where Have All the Apples Gone?

In the face of these facts, we must then ask where all the apples have gone. We need to look at why we have been reduced to fifteen varieties in 90 percent of the cases. We need to know what has happened to the other 16,985 varieties not represented in nearly all supermarkets.

The good news is that many varieties are still around. They are raised in small orchards and sold at roadside stands and farmers' markets. The bad news is that 13,000 varieties have disappeared forever and are no longer grown.

What killed these 13,000 varieties? Did some blight or mysterious disease sweep over the country in the early twentieth century?

The Industrialized Apple

The answer is very tragic. There was no blight. Mass markets killed these apple varieties.

When industrialization invaded agriculture at the beginning of last century, many small apple orchards, which were commonly part of small family farms, were pulled up. Only those varieties that could adapt well to industrial processes survived. Apples that were apt to bruise were not saved. Likewise, those which did not travel or store well were not valued. Still others failed to make the cut because they did not produce enough apples per tree.

Over time, the 17,000 varieties once grown were largely reduced to the fifteen. Even these survivors are not safe from the relentless search to engineer the perfect apple. The key word is "engineer" since this is a scientific exercise to maximize return on investment, not necessarily enhance the taste. New varieties like Cosmic Crisp are super-productive, store, and travel better. They are gradually replacing the big fifteen. Some scientists are even trying to develop varieties that reduce the time needed to produce mature trees from years to months.

What Was Lost

However, in the race to produce the most profit-efficient apple, much apple culture was lost. A way of life was lost as the landscape changed.

Apples once grew all over the country. Regarding culture, the regional character of consumption was altered since many of the lost varieties grew best in the area, its climate, and soil. Even the means of producing new varieties were lost, since many of these came about by the chance cross pollination of neighboring orchards. A local apple was prized by the inhabitants as their own and became part of the regional culture.

Even the names of varieties were picturesque and evocative of people and place. A 1905 book, *The Apples of New York*, lists numerous state varieties. We find Grimes Golden Apples described as "beautiful, rich, golden-yellow, attractive in form and excellent either for dessert or culinary use." There is the Winter Banana Apple which is "large, clear pale yellow with beautiful contrasting pinkish-red blush, characteristically aromatic, of good dessert quality." And what to think about the Twenty Ounce apple? It is "highly esteemed for home use, large, attractive, green becoming yellowish with broad strips and splashes of red, moderately tender, juicy."

These 17,000 different tastes enriched the American apple scene and developed a healthy regionalism. These same apples also figured in apple products that likewise enhanced a locale and its traditions. They would lend their distinctive flavors to all sorts of variations of apple cider, vinegar, butter, brandy, strudel, and the classic American apple pie.

It is amazing to think how much the simple apple added to our culture. It is sad to imagine how much was lost when the distinct flavors of 13,000 varieties have faded out of existence.

Not Only Apples

The influence of a product on culture is not limited to apples. In what can be called an organic society, there is a natural link between a locality, its people, and products. This is contrary to the frenetic intemperance of a society that focuses only on money and efficiency with no connection to a locality or its people.

Thus, we should imagine a whole society where distinctive local foods, clothes, and products are each represented by thousands of varieties. It is said, for example, that the flavor of local grit corn was so distinctive in the South that people could tell where they were by the taste of the grits.

No amount of marketing can replace truly organic foods that are rooted in a region and its tradition.

Did It Have to Happen?

Some might dismiss these considerations as nostalgic musings about the past that ignore modern-day reality. They claim that the market may be brutal but nevertheless must be respected.

We would respond that the devastation of apples did not need to happen the way it did. Local cultures could have flourished with full respect for markets. There are certain niche markets like craft beers that are proof that local production can be highly competitive.

Indeed, we must also recognize that massive centralized markets rarely operate on purely fair-market principles. Government subsidies, local tax-privilege packages, burdensome socialist regulations made to benefit big suppliers, and vast distribution systems have certainly helped keep markets gigantic to the detriment of the small producer.

A Moral, Not Economic, Problem

However, what devastated the apple market was much more a moral problem than an economic one. When people reject moral restraints and insist upon instant gratifications of their desires, it throws markets out of balance. It leads societies to forsake the natural restraining influence of family, faith, and community that keep economies refreshingly local and impressively stable.

The breakdown of family and community, especially since the sixties, played a major role in this devastation. When individuals are no longer anchored in families and communities, there can be no true local economy since it must rest upon the work of generations and a reverence for place. People without roots choose the product that is most convenient or inexpensive.

People with roots are loyal to them. They naturally prefer products with which they have a link and participation, as they are part of their history. People appreciate the distinctive local flavors that come from the soil, climate, or their own inventiveness.

Above all, true localism consists of the human element. People have the joy of living together and sharing the things they love...including apples. This is what gives rise to the cultural treasures so amazingly expressed by 17,000 apple varieties.

CHAPTER 4

Hotel #341, Forever Nowhere

BY JOHN HORVAT II

By maximizing efficiency, frenetic intemperance leads to the standardization and mechanization of life. This results in a situation in which everything around us starts to look and feel the same. This can be seen in the case of nationwide hotels and franchise. Materially, everything might be entirely clean, comfortable, and orderly. Material desires are satisfied, but spiritual wants are neglected. The human element is missing. The result is a frustratingly bland and impoverishing experience.

During some recent travel, I chanced to stay in a brand new hotel near a major American city. There was nothing extraordinary about the place. I had no complaints. The hotel was comfortable and clean, and these are evidently things that must be appreciated.

However, what bothered me was the fact that it was not connected to any one locality. It was as if a giant helicopter had dropped the whole building into a space and called it Hotel #341, and that further down the highway, an identical building was airlifted to a similar space and called Hotel #342.

As I looked out my window, this impression was confirmed by a patch of mangled trees and brush that seemed to reflect the impact of the dropped hotel. There was no attempt to connect this wild area to the well-manicured lawn that surrounded the hotel. There were no landmarks, save an unidentifiable highway in the distance, to help give some context as to where I was. Hotel #341 could be anywhere.

Inside Hotel #341, I felt as though I was in a pod insulated from the rest of the world. The rooms were hermetically sealed; the windows would not open. My room was nearly identical to those around me. All had the same decorations and supplies. In all the rooms, one could find those same meaningless modern art pictures that have no connection to time or place. I looked in vain for something that would distinguish my room from any other in this hotel or from the versions of this chain of hotels found down the highway. Save for a local directory of restaurants (many of them featuring the typically standardized chain restaurants) and other useful places, I could not find any references to where I was in America.

There is, however, a way out of Hotel #341. On the wall is mounted a large portal that takes you out. This is the flat screen television with a remote control that gives the resident the power to view hundreds of stations outside the hotel. Thus, it might be argued, the person can break away from the artificial world of Hotel #341 and vicariously experience an immense variety of entertainments and localities. However, it must be noted that, although there are many channels available, these choices are also all identical to the channels found in any nearby hotel.

Again it must be stressed that my stay was not uncomfortable. The staff was polite and helpful. Save for its sameness, there was nothing memorable about my stay.

Something obviously was missing. I did not sense that spontaneous and organic element that enters into things and delights the human spirit by its distinctness and novelty. I would have liked to have seen some attention, room decoration, or personal interest that would make the stay memorable. I did not find that connection to a locale that makes the wide world a marvelous and adventurous place, full of variety and beauty. I found Hotel #341, forever the same, forever nowhere.

If we are to return to order, we will need to reconnect with the places around us. We will need to insert the human element back into the economy and go beyond mass standardization. Despite all its material comforts, we must check out of Hotel #341.

CHAPTER 5

A City without a Soul

BY JOHN HORVAT II

This case from outside the United States is a good example of what we do not want for our nation. Frenetic intemperance creates a soulless society in which people naturally do not wish to live. This is the tragic case of a Chinese city that, despite having every material convenience, lacks life and charm. Massive government planning kills the all-important warm, human element that gives life, meaning, and character to things. Bureaucracy creates relationships that are machine-like and soulless.

Near the bustling industrial city of Tieling in northeastern China, there is a brand new city some six miles down the road called Tieling New City. The place has everything going for it. Visitors will find excellent infrastructure, government offices, schools, shopping centers, and apartment complexes. Land and labor costs are significantly lower than other areas of China. Tieling New City can now hold some 60,000 residents with projections of triple that number in the near future.

The city even won special recognition from the U.N. Human Settlements Program as an example of "providing a well-developed and modern living space." The only problem is that Tieling New City is virtually a ghost town with almost no inhabitants. It is a city without a soul.

Tieling New City is a brainchild of socialist planners who still run the nation with social engineering and old-fashioned communist corruption. These planners spent millions of yuan cleaning up marshland that had been used to dump untreated sewage. The logic was build first and populate later. The project also served as an economic stimulus project. To keep up the illusion of constant growth, China often artificially pumps up its economy by creating construction jobs. It has burned through money by throwing up a number of ghost cities like Tieling New City all over the country.

In typical Communist Chinese fashion, these cities are riddled with bad loans and deals crafted by corrupt officials who often trample on the rights of farmers and villagers forced to evacuate these areas. This inorganic top-down manner of creating a city out of thin air is a sure-fire formula for building a city without a soul—and Tieling New City truly has no soul. People simply don't want to live there. There is no community life. There is no history or warmth. People feel more comfortable in crowded Tieling, where they have links with friends, family, and place.

Visitors cannot help but get an eerie feeling of being in a corpse-city when, at night, row after row of apartment buildings remain dark and nearly empty, save for a few residents and security guards. The industrial park is not much better. This vacant complex was built to be bustling with some 15,000 employees. Once complete, it had only two firms sign contracts, one of which employs around fifteen people. Even with such dismal occupancy, there are still plans to double the park's size. There is also a warehouse center on the outskirts of town that is virtually unused. Security guard seems to be the only real career opportunity in town with a future.

Despite the lack of enthusiasm for Tieling New City, the socialist planners were not easily discouraged. They came up with a set of socialist plans and schemes to move in people. According to the Tieling government website, building the industrial park created 5,000 jobs for rural workers in 2012. However, officials were soon disappointed to learn that most of the workers found places to live outside the new city. Officials then thought they found the solution when they moved many government offices from Tieling to Tieling New City. However, most government workers just commute from their old homes rather than move to the inhospitable city.

Officials went a step further by closing schools in the old city and forcing some 50,000 students to go to brand new schools in the new city. They hoped (against all hope) that parents would move closer to the schools. Alas, the parents are staying put. Despite the place's outwardly pleasant appearance, they complain that the absence of community and services make the soulless city unlivable.

In the face of such obstacles, socialist planners now believe the problem can be solved by building even more facilities. According to *The Wall Street Journal* (8/9/13), the municipal government will be spending another $1.3 billion on new projects. Maybe, just maybe, officials reason, people will be attracted by an art gallery, a gymnasium, an indoor swimming pool, and another (empty) shopping center.

What central planners fail to realize is that either cities are built organically, or they will be empty shells. The most important components of the city are individuals, families, and communities, not warehouses, industrial parks, and shopping centers.

As noted in *Return to Order*, when people and families experience the exuberant element of life together in society, there springs forth "unique systems of art, styles of life, socio-political institutions, and economic models that differ from the rigid and soulless central planning and one-size-fits-all solutions so prized by socialists and bureaucrats."

Indeed, so many fail to consider this human element which is essential to a sound economy. As for the Chinese socialist planners at Tieling New City, they think that economic health can be bought by just injecting money into an area without any link to the inhabitants. Bring back family, morals, and institutions to a city, and it will acquire a soul. Until then, the world is doomed to continue building cities without them.

CHAPTER 6

Why I Side with the One Percent

BY JOHN HORVAT II

When frenetic intemperance enters into an economy, people are treated like numbers to be compiled into statistics and spreadsheets. The real causes of economic problems are ignored and one-size-fits-all "solutions" are imposed upon a people, often with grave consequences. Real economies need to consider real people.

Amid all the talk about economic inequality, I unabashedly take the side of the one percent. I know it may not be a popular position, but I nevertheless feel an obligation to make it known. Mind you, my defense of the one percent is balanced. I do not necessarily think they should be paid more, and certainly not less. Overall, I think the media and the political establishment has blown the whole affair completely out of proportion.

In all fairness, I should mention that the one percent I side with is not the same one percent—the billionaires and millionaires—that was the target of the rabid attacks by the Occupy Wall Street crowd some time ago. My one percent roughly represents those who earn the federal hourly minimum wage.

For all the brouhaha around the issue, I came upon the surprising fact that only around one percent of the American workforce earns exactly the federal minimum wage. According to figures from the U.S. Bureau of Labor Statistics, roughly 1.5 million hourly workers out of nearly 155 million job holders are among this select group. I know there are other "casual" worker groups, such as farm workers or babysitters that earn less than minimum wage, but the focus of the present debate is on this one percent, and so I will restrict myself to considering these workers.

Perhaps one of the strongest reasons why I support this one percent is because I was once part of their number. In my high school days, I labored earning a mere $2.25 an hour. My entry-level job helped me go to college and avoid student debt. My experience taught me the value of work and the need to save. Since I earned so few of them, I learned early in life to value each dollar—which was certainly worth a lot more back then.

Today, as I look at the present earners of the federal minimum wage, I see pretty much the same demographic. Teenagers make up 31 percent of all federal minimum wage earners. Over 55 percent are under the age of twenty-five. Young workers, like I was, are precisely those who need entry-level jobs, since they do not have the skills to compete for higher paying jobs.

Not only is the one percent young, but it is largely part-time employment. Some 51.5 percent work an average of twenty-nine hours or less each week. Less than a third work full-time and of these only 39 percent are men.

The media image of legions of graduate-degree workers desperately trying to support families on fast-food wages simply does not correspond to reality. Another illusion is that these workers are construction workers being paid substandard wages by greedy contractors. In fact, only one percent of the one percent (15,000) are construction workers earning minimum wage. Indeed, as everyone knows, most of these wage earners work in food preparation and similar services, requiring minimal skills—and less compensation.

Knowing the real facts and figures about minimum-wage earners makes me take up the defense of the one percent. The distortions of the left do not correspond to the reality of living, working Americans who need these jobs, as I did, to supplement income or enter the workforce. Like it or not, pushing the minimum wage upward necessarily drives the number of jobs downward.

I dislike the patronizing way the left treats the one percent like… well, one percent: a statistic to be manipulated at will. For all their talk about compassion, liberal legislators, inside the safety of their ample salaries, see these workers as if they were mere parts in their political machine. They believe that decreeing a one-wage-fits-all increase and or expanding government programs will solve all family financial problems—and attract voters. They can conceive no charity beyond that handed out by big government.

They fail to see that throwing money at problems does not solve them. More often than not, poverty is caused by broken families, promiscuous lifestyles, and poor consumer habits that mark the frenetic intemperance of our times. The best way out of poverty is a stable family where members work together to confront life's difficulties. The heart and soul of any economy is not found in labor statistics and wage indexes, but in the families and communities, which provide that all important mutual support and charity that money cannot buy.

That is why I side with the one percent. I believe the one-percenters should have the right to be treated like real people and not imaginary beings or statistics. Young people and teenagers should have the opportunity to use their limited skills as a means of pursuing their dreams. Part-time jobs should play a healthy role in a robust economy.

I do not deny that we are facing hard times and that there are people suffering economic hardships with present wages. However, let us deal with the real issues that are the cause of this poverty. I firmly believe that the path to a healthy economy will not be found in wage hikes or fancy programs, but in a return to a moral order that is the real foundation of any prosperity.

CHAPTER 7

Shutting Down the Other Gun Culture

BY JOHN HORVAT II

Frenetic intemperance is such a dominant force in our culture that many people will sacrifice their own convictions to keep the frenzy going. They will even support dangerous activities like a favorable portrayal of gun violence. This leads to those cultural contradictions that end up creating moral chaos inside the modern mind.

It suddenly occurred to me that something was wrong when I saw the gun debate ignited again as it always is with each new killing spree. Every time, we hear the same message. The public is invited to clamor for measures to control guns to stop the violence. We are told to pressure our politicians to have the courage to face the powerful gun lobby. We are urged to reject our "violent gun culture."

To be honest, there isn't much I can do personally to reject this "violent gun culture." My exposure is minimal—and I suspect it is the same with tens of millions of other Americans, gun owners and non-owners alike. Most are like me who very rarely handle a weapon. People I know who do handle arms often are usually quite discreet about it. They seem to understand the seriousness of carrying any gun—and are familiar with those very rare occasions when a gun might be needed for self-defense. To these owners, guns represent restraint. I have no problem with this gun culture, since its adherents act responsibly, rationally, and calmly.

It is telling that, despite the extreme ease with which a person can become a member of a major gun rights organization (just pay dues), no mass killers appear to have been members. Similarly, no mass killers have been found to be fervent Christians, family men, or owners of significant property.

When I see this uproar about guns, I think about a second gun culture that no one dares mention. It is this gun culture that I vehemently oppose. Unlike the first culture, I am and can be continuously exposed to it. It is in my face and found all over the media. The use of weapons in this culture is irresponsible, deadly—and incredibly supported by liberals—and yet, no one protests.

This second culture is defined by the plots and themes invariably found in Hollywood films and video games. It seems that every action film is full of guns, misuse of weapons, and gratuitous violence. In fact, I am exposed to more guns in one of these films than a full year of exposure to the first culture.

You see this culture in the chase scenes where characters shoot at each other without any regard for what is around them. These are trigger-happy cowboys (and cowgirls) ever ready to shoot anything that moves. The weapons they sport are semi-automatic pistols, automatic weapons, and yet more sophisticated arms that deaden the public sensibility to violence. No one complains about these characters that cling to their guns and wreak havoc on society. Daily, we are flooded with images of these irresponsible characters that pull out a firearm at a moment's notice. We are witnesses to dramatic deaths that bear little resemblance to real death. Film stars engage in the frenetic intemperance of a surreal world that acts upon impulse and brutal actions. They make killing look so easy and gratifying.

I don't understand why people have no problem with this unreal world that glamorizes the guns and glories in scenes of massive violence. I am especially appalled by bloody video games that make today's mass murder sprees look like cakewalks. There seems to be no problem with these bloody acts that would be illegal and criminal in the real world.

Such scenes from action films and video games represent not a single episode of mass murder. Rather, it is as if the same mass murder is committed millions of times inside theaters, homes, and mobile devices. Inside the minds of countless youth, they send a message that guns are the means to impose one's will upon others. Guns represent power. To lonely young men from fatherless families frustrated by their failure to be part of society, the gun is the ultimate platform and avenger.

The same liberals who decry the first culture have little problem accepting the second. Ironically, liberal actors and actresses who support gun control will play ruthless characters that gun down their opponents. The same liberals that call for drastic gun control measures fill the theaters showing these action thrillers. They will idolize the film stars who wield their weapons so irresponsibly.

Is it any wonder that we have those who act out their fantasies based on the unreal world on the screen? Isn't it time we, liberals and conservatives alike, publicly denounce this other gun culture that sends such a deadly message?

I am not saying that Hollywood and video games are the only causes of the mass-murder phenomenon. However, I believe this second gun culture plays a major role. What is particularly alarming is that the desire for the frenetic intemperance is so high that even safety is sacrificed on the altar of unrestraint.

CHAPTER 8

Advice to Graduating Millennials: Don't Jump the Ropes

BY JOHN HORVAT II

Frenetic intemperance causes a person to dislike any rules, prohibitions, and authorities that impose restraints. People with this mentality are extreme individualists that believe they should be able to do whatever they want. This is dangerous and ruinous to society. There must be rules and authority if society is to survive. These rules serve the common good and keep society in order.

As I walked down the aisle of the plane, I saw in the seat next to mine an amiable young fellow—a real live millennial. I was intrigued by the opportunity to talk.

Don't get me wrong, plenty of millennial-age young people cross my path. Most of them don't make a big deal about their "millennialness."

This particular fellow, however, was the real thing. He self-identified as a millennial in our introduction. Thankfully he self-identified as something he actually is and not that which he imagines himself to be. We at least had the foundation for some kind of rational discussion.

He was an archetypal millennial on his way to his sister's graduation at an Ivy League school. Here was one of those children of affluent parents who have enough money to claim money is not important. In his hand was the latest iPhone on which he texted, swiped, and scrolled as we got to know each other. He ended his sentences with a slight up-tone that signaled no real commitment to his views as he probed my own.

It did not take long to realize that he professed an extreme individualism of allowing people to do whatever they wanted without

© Balate Cristian Mircea | Dreamstime.com

Rules are need to keep order in society.

moral restraints. At the same time, he expressed frustration at the political process, which he believed should exist more to facilitate personal self-fulfillment than to promote the common good. Despite
everything, he was optimistic about the future since he thought the
millennials would overcome all these obstacles by bringing meaning
and purpose to American life.

Of course, as the conversation progressed, we got into those hot-
button issues that are rocking campuses and the nation: transgender
tyranny, micro-aggressions, self-identification, and morality. I expected
some political turbulence as we cruised comfortably at 32,000 feet, but
the bumps never came. It was a rather fluid debate in which we did
not dwell for long on any particular subject. We disagreed on many issues, but he did not defend his positions vehemently.

In fact, it was rather easy to persuade him that, since lying and stealing are universally considered wrong in all cultures, some notion of
natural law must exist. He had to admit that it was wrong to force people to act against their informed conscience as in the case of florists,
bakers, and others asked to service same-sex "marriages." We even
came to agree that things objectively exist and that reality can be
known. Thus, self-identifying does not change the nature of things.

I was pleased to see that my millennial did not agree with many of
the politically correct opinions the media claim he is supposed to uphold. He expressed irritation about diversity issues on campus. He
lamented how our culture makes fathers look like clowns, and was
writing a paper on what it means to be a man. His family and religion
meant a lot to him. I could not help but admire his sense of adventure
and idealistic desire to do something with meaning and purpose. I was
surprised at some of the "conservative" attitudes he expressed.

Perhaps the most disconcerting part of the whole exchange was his
lack of certainty. Our friendly conversation was not like the passionate
student arguments of yore when people fought for their positions.

Our disagreements were much more temperamental than logical.
Uncertainty and insecurity informed his every thought. If he could not
explain something, he called it the product of evolution and social con-
structs. His temperamental resentment toward limits and restraints,
and the authority that imposes them, proved difficult to get around. I
wondered if there was any chance of introducing certainty into his
fluid world. I am not saying all millennials are like my fellow passenger,

only that the world that swirls around them favors the attitudes that my millennial had swallowed.

At a certain point, our discussion ended, and we each took to reading. As the flight came to a close, I engaged in a bit of small talk to pass the time. I found out that he liked to ski and, as one who has never skied, I asked him if it is difficult. He replied that it was not that hard as long as you didn't "jump the ropes."

I asked him what he meant by "jumping the ropes." He explained that there were certain areas of the mountain that are very dangerous because of the way the snow falls on them. If a person enters and skis these areas, it can cause an avalanche that can result in the death of the offender and those in the area. That is why, he explained, those in charge of the ski resorts rope off the dangerous areas and warn that those who venture into them do so at their own risk and should not expect to be rescued. Emphatically, he cautioned: "You don't want to jump the ropes."

As we each went our ways, I could not help but think about this last piece of advice and smile. In one sentence, he had summarized the whole point of our debate. With full certainty, he had affirmed the need for restraints, and the right of authority to establish limits. He acknowledged the tragic consequences of what happens when there are no ropes. He was clear, compelling, and reasonable.

On his part, I am sure he went to his sister's graduation ceremony and heard a politically correct commencement address that urges

© Roman Lysogor | Dreamstime.com

Venturing into forbidden areas can trigger an avalanche.

graduates to accept no limits—not even the restraints of identity and nature. This is not the message they need to survive in the real world. If I were asked to give some advice to graduating millennials, I would stick to the words of my flight companion: Pursue a life of purpose and meaning, but don't jump the ropes, lest you trigger an avalanche.

CHAPTER 9

The Emperor Is Wearing Pajamas: The Decline of Dress

BY JOHN HORVAT II

A dramatic example of frenetic intemperance is the revolution in fashion that has turned everything upside down. The logic of today's fashion is that dress must be comfortable and should not conform to any rules dictated by society. The result is an everything-goes world in which people dress to be like everyone else. The only thing not fashionable is propriety and modesty. Today, some are even wearing pajamas in public.

The modern attitude toward dress is that it has little effect on the way people function. In fact, people are advised that the more comfortable they are, the more efficient and happy they will be. People generally respond to such advice by collectively retreating into a shabby array of blue jeans or shorts, T-shirts or sweatshirts, and sneakers. It does not make any difference what you wear. It is all a matter of personal preference.

Such conclusions do not coincide with those who study attire. They have always affirmed that clothes are more than just covering. What one wears has an effect on what one does or how one performs. Educators notice a change in performance when students wear uniforms. Soldiers fight better when they know how to maintain the sharpness of their dress uniforms. Businessmen get better results when in formal attire. Clothes express one's personality and individuality; they communicate who the person is.

A study co-authored by Prof. Michael Kraus of the Yale School of Management provided a noteworthy proof of the effect of clothes in the business world. He found that wearing clothes of high social status greatly influenced job performance and communicated a note of dominance and mastery to those engaged in negotiations.

Prof. Kraus compared the results of two groups of men, one wearing business suits and dress shoes, and another in sweatpants, T-shirts, and plastic sandals. Those in the two groups were told to negotiate the

sale of a hypothetical factory and were given leeway to make conces-
sions. The men in suits conceded an average of $860,000 off the list
price of the factory as compared with concession of $2.81 million for
those in the sweatpants. The researchers found that those better-
dressed behaved with more control; they elicited more respect and ex-
uded more confidence.

Similar results were reported in a study in the journal *Social Psychological and Personality Science*. People in formal business attire proved
more capable of high levels of abstract thinking. They tended to see
the big picture more easily than casual dressers. This made them more
successful in their business decisions since they did not get bogged
down in useless detail.

The moral of the story is not that everyone should always wear formal business attire on all occasions. The real moral is that each type
of clothing is suited for a purpose for which it is designed. Sweat-
panted executives and suited runners are signs of a world gone awry.
When people ignore purpose in clothes, it has consequences.

Deep down everyone knows that clothes make a difference. The evidence is irrefutable. Yet so many bizarre fashions still dominate.

Part of the blame for this disregard of function in clothes can be laid
on the fashion world. Designers make it a point to overturn every
taboo and convention in their search for novelty, excitement, and fri-
volity. The fashion world creates enormous pressure on people to follow the fads or else be ostracized.

The result is fashions that contradict common sense. In what might
be called the frenetic intemperance of wearing whatever fashion dic-
tates, there is a callous disregard for function in clothes. It leads to a
corresponding desire to destroy propriety and modesty. People become self-absorbed by their own comfort and unconcerned about how
they might appear to others.

To cite yet one more example, there is a new high-fashion trend now
invading public spaces and social life. It is the wearing of pajamas as a
form of social attire. Man-style bottom and top pajamas are finding
their way into places outside the bedroom. Fashion houses are now
selling out of designer pajamas made to replace evening gowns and
cocktail dresses at formal social gatherings. Well-known celebrities
have been appearing publicly in pajamas and even bedroom slippers
to give yet more prestige to the trend.

The problem is pajamas look like...well, pajamas. They are not made for social life. They rightly project the untidy image of people who are ready for sleep or who have just awoken. Pajamas presuppose an intimacy with loved ones that cannot be shared by the general public—yet the fashion world has decreed that pajamas are chic, and people must therefore obey.

Even the fashion designers have a hard time overcoming the bizarreness of sleepwear in the public square. They recommend that their striped pajamas be paired with other fashion accessories like dressy shoes, belts, or blazers, perhaps to blunt the shocking impression of one being a prison escapee. Pajama pants on the street are marketed as "sleep pants" so as to appear more like a distant and laid-back cousin of sweat pants. Designers admit that daytime pajamas represent a "rebellious spirit" that is not for the faint-hearted.

All this is part of a general disorder in fashion in which suits are belittled and pajamas exalted. A day will come when people will be freed from the chains of the *fashionistas*. When that return to order happens, people will dress once again with purpose, modesty, and beauty. Until then, people will continue to appear in an embarrassing and bizarre array of clothes (or lack of clothes), awaiting the "Eureka!" moment when some innocent child will cry, "The emperor is wearing the wrong clothes!"

CHAPTER 10

Answering a Troubling Question: Man, Woman, or Whatever?

BY JOHN HORVAT II

Frenetic intemperance causes people to flee from restraints—even the most obvious ones. There is no denying that certain logical, biological, and existential truths stand in the way of unrestraint. One of these truths is the biological distinction of sex into male and female. Such a roadblock, however, is overcome by just turning reality into fantasy. Fantasy allows the imagination to be free, but it is also the worst tyrant when people try to run a society based on it.

A friend of mine recently rejoiced because he had finally found a job after being unemployed for a few months. It was an engineering job with a good company comparable to the one he had held before. However, there was one thing about the final interview that bothered him. He was asked, "What is your gender?"

My friend is an outdoorsman with a wife and children. It is evident that he is the man he is, so he was understandably offended and embarrassed at the same time. He was perplexed that this query was presented as a serious question that he had to answer for a job that is all about physical, observable reality. The fact that it is now part of the standard operating procedures of a reputable engineering firm is a disturbing omen of terrible things to come.

Worse yet, I can imagine that some liberal readers might even look with sympathy upon the question that I view as troubling since they see it as somehow making amends for the centuries of "oppression" suffered by those who think themselves transgendered—long before the term or notion was invented. Such sympathizers have always prepared the way for the acceptance of absurd trends.

Confusion about one's sex is a sign of our times.

The simple fact is that this question did not just happen. It is the fruit of a long process. It also points to the appearance of future existential questions that will cast doubt on just about anything.

We can take the sexual revolution of the sixties as a point of departure for what we are experiencing. This revolution sought to install a culture that leads people to resent the very idea of restraint, and scorn the spiritual, religious, moral, and cultural values that serve to order and keep society in balance. It declared that all morality is a mere "construct" of society that can be and should be "deconstructed" to make room for new levels of freedom.

As a result, the sexual revolution has done much to break down the barriers between the sexes. It has ushered in a wave of promiscuity that has led to the proliferation of divorce, contraception, abortion, premarital sex, homosexuality, unmarried couples, and pornography everywhere. All this has contributed to destroying society's moral fiber and mainstreaming every type of sexual disorder. It has to a large extent, succeeded in obtaining this particular goal.

We are suffering the consequences of this revolution in the tragedies of shattered lives, broken families, and empty churches that litter the social landscape and are tearing the nation apart. The "freedom" offered by the sexual revolution has yielded disastrous consequences that weigh heavily upon all society and the public purse.

However, even with the generalizing of promiscuity since the sixties, it proved impossible to be rid of all restraints. Those who pushed forward the sexual agenda had to admit the undeniable physical reality that the male and female categories still exist and carry with them their respective restrictions. They still had to work inside the complex parameters of a male/female world.

Moreover, inside this male/female reality, there always exists the possibility of forming a family and the re-establishment of a morality that would undermine the "gains" of the sexual revolution. That is why this next phase of the sexual revolution—the transgender revolution—is so threatening and bizarre. The agents of this change need no longer be anchored in physical reality, logic, or biological science. Reality becomes what you imagine it to be. In such a fantasy world, one can ignore the obvious and ask: Are you a man? Woman? Something in between?

That is to say, we have entered the reign of fantasy where concrete reality is forced to conform to delusions. This is not the action of some isolated, confused, and attention-seeking individuals who do not affect the population as a whole. No, the official business establishment is now institutionalizing fantasy and making it part of their reality. It involves schools, universities, and government institutions that are abolishing sexual pronouns, inventing new ones, and penalizing those who make mistakes in their use.

That is the troubling part of the question. No society can function inside such a framework of fantasy. Modernity is based on a rational foundation and a materialism that needs predictability, statistics, and real-time data to work efficiently. Since fantasy abstracts from logic, it must use force to compel people to adhere to its erratic and irrational rules. When the obvious man can no longer be considered a man and the obvious woman can no longer be considered a woman, fantasy rules. Any new imagining (beyond transgenderism) can become the norm. That is dangerous, for fantasy is the stuff upon which tyranny is built.

In the face of such an irrational revolution, we must resist the pressure to start thinking in terms of fantasy. Indeed, how would you answer the troubling question?

Why College Students Are Using Coloring Books

BY JOHN HORVAT II

One of the natural consequences of frenetic intemperance is stress. When people defy the limits of their human nature, it causes the breakdown of that calm and deliberating demeanor proper to balanced individuals. This is particularly the case among youth who are always pressured to embrace the newest and most bizarre lifestyles and practices in the name of fashion and fads. Universities are scrambling to find ways to coddle students when they should be forming character and preparing students for the hardships of life.

The present climate at the nation's universities has led people to expect almost anything from academia. There are safe spaces that resemble adult playpens where students can shield themselves from "micro-aggressions." There are trigger warnings to help students protect their politically correct sensitivities from free speech. Now... there are college-student coloring books.

That's right. College coloring books with colored pencils or felt pens are now the rage as administrators scramble to find ways to help students de-stress. Ironically, students that break all the rules at campus protests find solace in staying within the lines. The old-fashioned coloring book, perhaps one of the few undigitized things left, is going viral. Students, who try to pass themselves off as 21-year-olds to drink alcohol, are eager to assume the role of 5-year-olds when it is time to bring out the crayons.

This is not a marketing fad like the adult coloring book rage. Rather, official university policy is fueling the student coloring experience. These are not isolated colleges, but campuses nationwide including Ivy League schools. While there is yet to appear a Coloring 101 course, university employees are the ones handing out the coloring books and holding "coloring events" on campus.

American University, for example, provided coloring sheets on campus, explaining on its Facebook page how coloring "can help with a number of emotional and mental health issues." The Facebook page of

Crayons, once limited to kindergartens, are now found at colleges.

U.C. San Diego reported on "De-Stress Coloring Nights" before finals with all materials provided. In 2015, Brown University offered coloring books (and Play-Doh) in all its "safe space" rooms. The University of Missouri handed out an official Mizzou Coloring Book at its student union. The University of Nebraska-Omaha organizes regular De-Stress Fests at the university library with large turnouts. All of this is done in the name of therapy.

However, college officials have got it wrong in offering this therapy. The purpose of university education is not meant to be therapeutic, but formative. The university is supposed to form character in students and prepare them for adulthood and family life. Students should be exposed to a philosophy of education where they are taught to confront reality and overcome obstacles they will find when they live in the real world. The university should be a place of culture where the classic insights of the great thinkers of the past can benefit the present. College should mark a farewell to childhood and childish things. It should be the ex-hilarating embrace of independence and adult responsibilities.

Instead, many modern universities have adopted a philosophy in which the college coloring book is but a sad sign of the times. It is the fruit of a Hollywood culture that resists the natural need to grow up and assume responsibility. Many students aim to live forever-young lives of frenetic intemperance, in which they are encouraged to desire everything—instantly and effortlessly.

They defer major decisions about what they are to do with their lives and see college as a mere extension of their adolescence...or perhaps now a regression to kindergarten. When young people fail to live up to the responsibilities proper to their age group, they will indeed become stressed. Hence, the recourse to the therapeutic coloring books.

However, the coloring-book issue is also symptomatic of a university system that has lost touch with its purpose. The chief objective of the university should be the teaching of truth and its applications to life. Modern universities have strayed from this great mission largely because so many believe there is no truth. Indeed, the truth has become whatever one believes it to be at the moment. Values are whatever one happens to value, and a person is whatever he/she/it self-identifies as.

In short: Everything is fluid, constructed, and subjective. In modern academia, there is no objective truth or any applications of that truth. There are only isolated experiences disconnected from truth. Students are immersed in what Notre Dame Professor Brad Gregory has called "the kingdom of whatever." The university has gone from the search for eternal truth to the pursuit of personal experiences, from the consideration of forever to the acceptance of "whatever."

"Whatever" schooling undermines the purposes of education: character formation and the teaching of truth. It will naturally frustrate and cause anxiety. Instead of finding a divinely ordered universe bristling with variety and purpose, students are presented a sterile, godless universe devoid of meaning. Is it any wonder that they are offered fantasy-filled coloring books in which they might color their own "whatever" worlds?

Of course, the descent from classics to coloring books appears absurd to most people with common sense. It seems like a bad dream in need of a rude awakening—but it is not a dream. It is happening. The tragedy is that students will find out all too soon that the only way to deal with life's vicissitudes is to confront reality, not to color it away.

CHAPTER 12

Why Johnny Can't Sled Anymore

BY JOHN HORVAT II

The natural and organic ways in which children learn to deal with life are being destroyed. In their place, the modern world proposes violent fantasy models that come from frenetic intemperance and hinder the proper development of children.

On a cold winter afternoon, I chanced to come upon a scene that gladdened my heart. It was a group of unsupervised boys sledding down a hillside. They weren't only sledding. They were ramming into other sleds. At the bottom of the hill, they pushed each other down, rolling and tumbling in the snow. They threw snowballs at each other, all the while yelling and carrying on. The boys were just being boys, having a good old time in the process. I was thoroughly entertained by the spectacle, remembering scenes from my own youth.

"Dangerous" activities like sledding help children learn how to deal with small risks so they can deal with real dangers later on in life.

I was also edified by what I saw because in that scene there were all sorts of lessons being taught outside the politically correct classroom. Here were boys joyfully defying the gender police by naturally exhibiting that aggressive and manly behavior that makes them different from girls. I saw them developing and honing social skills like conflict management and alliance making. In the rough and tumble, the boys also learned that acts have consequences that sometimes hurt and require one to measure risks and avoid undue dangers. In that short episode in their exuberant lives, the boys learned about life with all its joys and sufferings.

The scene also saddened me with the fact that such scenes are becoming ever rarer. The lessons are deliberately left untaught. Boys must no longer be stereotyped as boys (even though they *are* boys). Thus, they are told they should not engage in rough play and scuffles. It is better to be tethered to electronic devices which are considered much safer than zipping down hills. This conclusion hit home when I read that many cities all over the country are banning sledding at public parks. It's just too dangerous. They are also closing down the hills because of liability concerns.

Cities like Dubuque and Des Moines, Iowa; Lincoln, Nebraska; and Columbia City, Indiana, now prohibit or restrict sledding on public property. In Paxton, Illinois, officials even went to the point of bulldozing down its sledding hill to keep playful children off.[1] Many cities have been hit with multi-million dollar lawsuits from sledding accidents.

Of course, children can be injured by sledding. No one denies this fact. Children can be injured in any kind of intense physical activity, but the likelihood that any one of the nation's 75 million children will be injured by sledding is measured in the low hundredths of a percent, many of which will be minor incidents. Such accidents are part of growing up. It does not exclude tragic accidents which will always be with us, since no civilization has ever been able to eliminate them.

However, "dangerous" activities like sledding serve a purpose. When children are exposed to small dangers, they then know how to deal with real ones when they confront them later on in life. They learn how to gauge the risks involved and react accordingly. They need to learn from a very early age that acts have consequences that often hurt. Parents do their children no favors when they seek to eliminate all reasonable risks from their paths. They fail to see that the innocent fun found in sledding or rough physical activities connects the child to reality and helps him deal with future problems in a natural and organic way.

The real tragedy is that today's youth are offered a contrary program. Instead of sledding, many children are often exposed to the frenetic intemperance of alternatives that help them disconnect from reality. While other children are "dangerously" playing in the snow, they will be engaged in video games that are full of all sorts of violent and risky

---

1. Cf. http://www.news-gazette.com/news/local/2013-02-20/paxton-park-board-removing-sledding-hill.html.

activities—and have no concrete consequences. They are free to gun down, run down, and mow down anyone in their path to gain points or advance the game. While others play unsupervised, these "safe" children will often be watching—alone and unsupervised—movies and programs full of violence, profanity, and sexual encounters—all at the click of a mouse. With such "lessons" being taught, should parents wonder why their children cannot deal with life's problems?

Overprotected from the real world, these unfortunate children are immersed in an unreal world where boys cannot be boys, and girls cannot be girls. All must be safe and sterile. Every physical risk is avoided while every moral danger is embraced and marked by an intolerable tolerance. Such a world stifles wonder and spontaneity. Indeed, it is a dangerous world when Johnny cannot sled anymore.

CHAPTER 13

Why Did Steve Jobs Limit His Children's Exposure to Technology?

BY JOHN HORVAT II

Frenetic intemperance is especially evident in the abusive use of technology that tends to dominate people's lives. Exposure to this technology is happening at an ever earlier age. Some people claim this exposure is positive since this technology represents the future. However, others, including parents working in high-tech industries, believe this exposure suppresses the child's creativity and development.

There is the mistaken impression that computers represent the future and that everyone, especially the very young, should become computer savvy as soon as possible. According to this view, failure to expose children to high technology handicaps their ability to function in the real world.

However, in the real world, addiction to the omnipresent small screens can be a handicap. Discouraging overexposure to technology might be an advantage in today's hyper-connected world.

Such views are not those of overprotective parents unfamiliar with these technologies. Even the most enthusiastic promoters of computer gadgetry can be seen discouraging the very products they produce. The most notable case was Apple co-founder Steve Jobs, who claimed he did not let his teenage children have iPads, and limited their tech consumption at home.

When the iPad exploded into the market in 2010, Jobs' daughters, Erin and Eve, were not part of the market. The late Steve Jobs and wife, Laurene Powell, deliberately regulated their children's exposure to the new products and its culture.

What did the young Jobs girls do instead of texting and surfing the Web? Apparently, they did the things normal children do.

Biographer Walter Isaacson reports the family had dinner together every night where they would discuss books, history, and other non-technical things. The iPad, iPhone, and other devices had no place at their table—and the children did not seem particularly disturbed by the fact.

Jobs, who died in October 2011, thought that limiting his daughters' computer use would help his children develop a love for creative expression. He did not want them whiling away their time on games and useless programs. Paradoxically, Jobs enthusiastically filled the world with gadgets that transformed the way most people listen to music, entertain themselves, and communicate. However, what he marketed to other families he did not necessarily want for his own.

Apparently, Jobs was not alone.

It appears that a growing number of high-tech executives take measures to limit the amount of exposure their children have to the technology they produce, design, and market. These concerned parents cite the new technology's overwhelming attraction and addiction as factors in their decisions.

One example of this trend is found at a Silicon Valley elementary school. According to a 2011 *New York Times* story on the trend, many engineers and executives from high-profile tech companies like Apple, eBay, Google, Hewlett-Packard, and Yahoo send their children to a Waldorf elementary school in Los Altos, California, where television viewing is discouraged, and electronic devices are banned. They claim such radical educational measures are necessary to ensure that their children develop all their talents without unnecessary distractions.

The computer should not be a child's best friend.

Such "radical" measures are not that radical. In fact, parents need not send their children to expensive private schools to allow their children the same privileges as their counterparts in Los Altos. All parents need to do is let their children be children. Children need to grow up being children with all the interacting, creativity, and spontaneity that has always been part of a healthy childhood. They need to do things like play games, eat together as a family, and solve problems together.

The real radicals are those who allow their children to be electronically sequestered and tethered to their little devices, and thus never encountering the real world. If there is any doubt about this, all one needs to do is ask the experts. Steve Jobs would agree.

God and the Double BBQ Sandwich

BY JOHN HORVAT II

Frenetic intemperance is also a point of division in America. The context of the debate over the future of our nation has often been expressed in political or economic terms. Perhaps there is another way of expressing this polarized situation. What we have are two visions of society in conflict. One of these is attached to an America that is attracted to supernatural and metaphysical values. The other is linked to frenetic intemperance.

It is no secret that America is polarized. This is a fact that is manifested in so many different ways. Traveling down the highway to Chicago, for example, I came upon two successive billboards that I thought were striking examples of our divided culture.

The first billboard caught me by surprise: It consisted of an electro-cardiogram of a heart that suddenly stops beating. The caption read, "When you die, you will meet God."

As we were passing through the snowy night, I was unable to catch more details of this billboard. I do not know who put it out or what I was expected to do. It did not matter because for a brief moment, I thought about what the Catholic Church calls the "Four Last Things": Death, Judgment, Heaven, and Hell. "Think of these things," Scripture says, "and you will not be lost eternally." The simple phrase served to trigger in me a gentle yet fleeting reflection upon the meaning of life. I am sure I was not the only one to make this quick reflection.

The billboard is polarizing since it is directed toward that strong vein inside the American public that is turned toward things religious, spiritual, and eternal. It is a sector of the American public that lives amid the fast, superficial, and materialistic aspects of our pop culture, yet is not entirely comfortable with them. These Americans are drawn by God, family, honor, and country. On the other hand, this billboard would not appeal to other Americans who would tend to disparage the message as backward and unenlightened.

The second billboard came immediately afterward and struck me by how contrary it was to the former. It consisted of a massive BBQ sandwich with the caption, "Happiness is a Double BBQ Sandwich."

There is nothing wrong with a double BBQ sandwich or even deriving pleasure from eating one. However, the message behind this billboard is materialistic, yet more subtly polarizing. There is no invitation to profound reflection. Rather, there is the quick insinuation that happiness can be easily bought by obtaining the immediate object of our desires. In this case, gratification equals happiness. According to the same logic, life should be a long succession of gratifications.

This billboard represents a second, more commercial vein found in America that believes the nation is organized like a co-op. This perspective holds that individuals unite themselves together in society as a means to facilitate each one's inebriating pursuit of happiness.

Under this view, an appreciation of America is tied to its ability to make everything fun and everyone happy. Like a co-op, those who hold this position expect returns on their social union in the form of constant and instant gratification. Happiness consists of participating in the excitement of a party economy that they hope will keep on going.

Of course, we cannot generalize and say that all Americans fit neatly into one category or the other. Sometimes the two can be found in differing proportions inside the same person. Sometimes, the person might gravitate toward one, later to the other. We might also observe collective swings of the national mood towards one or the other category.

As our crisis deepens, this fascinating interplay of perspectives, this dramatic clash of mentalities becomes the material for a great debate now taking place in America over our future. This discussion is found everywhere—even on highway billboards.

There are many categories that people have used to characterize the nation's polarization. There is red and blue, conservative and liberal, retro and metro. Perhaps it is the case to add yet another: God and the double BBQ sandwich.

PART II THE FOUNDATION OF AN ORGANIC ORDER: ORGANIC SOLUTIONS

T he preceding examples of frenetic intemperance are far from exhaustive. We could have developed other themes that stress more the abuse of technology and the creation of a gigantic and impersonal world that has harmful effects on individuals and society. Our treatment, however, does establish that a frenetically intemperate society is undesirable and that we need to find alternatives.

Such solutions can be found in what we call an organic Christian society. It corresponds to the natural development of man and society that will lead to an economy and culture without frenetic intemperance. It is a social order oriented towards the common good that naturally and spontaneously develops under the guidance of the principles of natural law and the Gospel, thus allowing man to pursue the perfection of his essentially social nature.

However, in our days of frenetic intemperance, the concept of organic society is abstract and hard to imagine. Its many manifestations require stories and examples that make them clear.

We will start our exposition of organic society with what we call "organic solutions." The fundamental principle behind them is simple: We must seek to discover basic principles associated with the nature of things and in accordance with the Gospel, and then allow enormous freedom in their application to the needs of the person or society. We need not limit ourselves to a single system, but allow a vast variety of legitimate solutions that adapt to the inequality found in men, peoples, and circumstances of life.

As *Return to Order* points out, "Organic society gives us a few general rules from which come thousands of systems. Socialism gives us one system from which comes a thousand rules and regulations. From this, we can conclude that it is much more important to have the right general rules and principles than to design a rigid, one-size-fits-all system."

Like "*Return to Order* moments," organic solutions often appear naturally and unexpectedly. In this section, we will present examples of products, services, and other things that are the fruit of following a few rules and then allowing enormous freedom in applying them. The range of these organic solutions is almost inexhaustible. As can be seen from the examples, they have already enriched our American society, nourishing the desires people have for authentic regionalism.

What My Medieval Calendar Taught Me at a Modern Airport

BY JOHN HORVAT II

Organic solutions do not have to be sophisticated. Sometimes they can be very primitive, almost medieval. These unexpected solutions run contrary to the fashions and fads that are often artificial and pre-planned. The world of frenetic intemperance gives the impression that everyone must use the latest fashion or be considered outdated and inefficient. This is not true. In fact, organic solutions are refreshing, imaginative, and more common than we think.

I was sitting in the airport with plenty of time on my hands. Unlike those around me, I did not have an electronic device to entertain me. To make matters worse, I had forgotten to bring the book I was reading, and so I took out my calendar to see what needed to be done or scheduled.

As I was busy with my calendar, I was surprised by the man sitting next to me who suddenly exclaimed, "Hey, that's a pretty nice calendar you have there!"

My calendar, I should explain, is a three-ring notebook with lined pages. I divide the pages by manually drawing vertical lines to separate the days of the week. Inside these divisions are notes of the things I need to do, boxes with agendas for meetings, or just reminders that keep me on schedule. It is a very primitive, almost medieval arrangement, but I have found it to be very flexible. It developed organically and allows all sorts of changes to accommodate what I need to do.

The man who had just praised my calendar was someone approaching sixty, in casual business attire, and gave the impression of being a professional or executive. That he would compliment my calendar was the last thing I would have expected from him.

I asked him why he liked my calendar and he replied, "Because I have one just like it. I thought I was the only one that has something like yours. Now I am happy to see that there are others like me."

I was also surprised since I had thought the same thing, that I was the only one to do something so different. I was under the mistaken impression that anyone wanting to be part of the real world had to have some fancy scheduling program or app.

Nevertheless, this man obviously was part of the real world. He later explained to me that he was a fashion artist in New York City. He also has a large farm in Missouri that he had inherited. He now manages it and thus frequently visits. He was a very busy man who had a very busy schedule . . . and a very primitive calendar.

We started talking shop. I explained a few of my secrets and showed him some pages with my past weeks' schedules. He chimed in with a few tips on how he did things. We both commented on how technology does not solve all scheduling problems, and sometimes even makes things worse. Much more important than the devices and programs are the scheduling habits that you develop. You don't need to follow all the latest high-tech fads and gadgets. Sometimes all that is needed is a bit of common sense to find the system that works best for you.

At a certain point in the conversation, I decided to up the ante and see how far I might go with this train of thought.

I pulled out my ancient Samsung flip-phone that looked so twentieth century. He immediately took out his outdated and dilapidated Blackberry that he assured me was cutting-edge primitive without any bells or whistles. We both agreed that so many of the new devices can be very superfluous and time-consuming. It is easier to get by using what you truly need.

I learned two lessons from the airport conversation. The first was that not everybody follows all the latest fads. There are many like my friend, who do not go along with the frenetic intemperance of buying every gadget or app that appears on the market. They use the technology they need even if it might seem outdated. They believe that we should not serve technology, but that technology should serve us. I learned that we should not be afraid to resist the trends that often dictate how we should act.

The second lesson was that organic solutions that we develop ourselves are often the best ones. They stand out and are so refreshing in a world where everything is so artificially organized and pre-planned. I am sure there are many like my friend at the airport, who develop imaginative solutions that would delight and surprise us. I am certain we can find examples of these organic solutions everywhere if we just take the time and trouble to look. Indeed, this is something I would like to study more in depth. I think I will put it on my medieval calendar.

CHAPTER 16

America's Native Spirit

BY NORMAN FULKERSON

The origin and tradition of Kentucky bourbon is a charming example of organic solutions. All the right factors came together almost haphazardly to create a world-renowned product. Even more important than the actual drink is the human element that is always part of organic solutions. When people and families come together and dedicate themselves to excellence, great things happen... and great bourbons are born.

It might appear to a casual observer that the United States is not a country where one would find a healthy regionalism. Nowhere is this more apparent than in the Bluegrass State, which is commonly seen merely as the home of Kentucky Fried Chicken. Those who see it this way might be surprised to learn that a centuries-old tradition of producing world-class bourbon found its origin right here in tiny Nelson County, Kentucky.

It was a particularly picturesque morning as I drove down the Bluegrass Parkway across rolling hills towards Bardstown, Kentucky. The sun peeped below a low-lying mist and cast a marvelous bronze hue across the frost-covered landscape. This is the heart of Kentucky's Bourbon Trail, and the dream-like color of the countryside that day seemed identical to the wonderful liquid which has put it on the world map. This idyllic morning, I would later find out, revealed a profound symbolism; that which makes Kentucky bourbon so extraordinary has as much to do with the soil from which it is born as the people who harness its potential for excellence. This is what gives it such a refreshing, regional character.

Generations of Kentuckians have continued the heritage and time-honored tradition of making fine bourbon.

"A region," according to John Horvat in his book *Return to Order*, "is formed by the intimate relationship between a people and a place." He goes on to point out how such a place has its "own vegetation, lay of the land, natural wonders, hinterland, and mysteries."[1]

This is what one can see in this geographic region of the Bluegrass State called Old Bourbon, which sits atop a massive, six-county-wide limestone shelf. This calcium filters out the unwanted iron, turning it into the ideal water for bourbon. Curiously enough, it is the same bone-strengthening water that is a contributing factor in producing million-dollar racehorses and explains why Kentucky's numerous distilleries are intertwined with finely manicured thoroughbred farms.

The other element that must not be overlooked is the white oak trees native to this region that are used to make barrels for aging bourbon. During the hot, humid Kentucky summers, the bourbon expands into the walls of the barrel. In the cold winter, it retracts, taking with it a variety of flavors—anything from vanilla, caramel, to fruity or citrus notes and... the marvelous amber color.

Lastly, it's Kentucky's fertile soil that produces an abundance of another essential ingredient: corn. For it to be called bourbon, there has to be at least 51 percent corn in the mash.

"Sometimes it seems that there are places that Providence has blessed with harmonic features," Mr. Horvat continues, "as if awaiting inhabitants."[2]

Everything necessary to make excellent bourbon was put in place for just such people, and their arrival would occur in an unexpected way.

The Origins of "Old Bourbon"

It all began with the Whiskey Rebellion of 1791 when George Washington imposed an excise tax on the domestic manufacture of all spirits. Disgruntled European immigrants—primarily Scots, Irish, and Germans—were furious over what they considered an unjust levy on a product they brought from the Old World, and decided to pack up and head south to the fledgling Commonwealth of Kentucky. They eventually settled in Bourbon County, named after the French royal

---

1. John Horvat II, *Return to Order: From a Frenzied Economy to an Organic Christian Society—Where We've Been, How We Got Here, and Where We Need to Go* (York, Penn.: York Press, 2013), 205.

2. Ibid.

family. This county was later carved into many smaller ones, but many people continued to call the whole region "Old Bourbon." Located within its boundaries was the principal Ohio River port of the same name from which whiskey and other products were shipped south.[3]

They recommened making their fine whiskey, but when they sent it down the Ohio and Mississippi Rivers to New Orleans in oak barrels, a curious thing happened. The long trip aged the whiskey, thus enhancing its taste profile, while the oak wood gave the drink its distinct mellow flavor and trademark color. The recipients of this unique spirit enjoyed it very much but were curious as to what it was called. Seeing "Old Bourbon" stenciled on the barrels—to indicate their port of origin—they began calling it "bourbon."

This was the organic beginning of a liquor that would go on to earn the name "America's Native Spirit."[4]

Since then, generations of Kentuckians have continued the heritage and time-honored tradition of making fine bourbon, unchanged from the process used by their ancestors. It has become an international symbol of Kentucky craftsmanship and tradition, which has attracted nearly two million visitors from around the world in the last five years alone.[5]

Bourbon "Nobility"

One name that is indisputably linked to the industry is Jacob Beam's. After immigrating to America from Germany in the eighteenth century, he started his first distillery in 1788 with a unique strain of yeast, which he carefully guarded against the hot summers by placing it in a jug, then depositing it in a nearby creek to keep cool. He would go on to teach his son everything he knew about making bourbon, and they, in turn, passed on the knowledge to their sons and grandsons.

A youthful and bubbly Erica Boone was my tour guide the day I visited this historic distillery. She is proud of being a descendant of Daniel Boone, but her face glowed with pride when she named another of her ancestors. "I am an eight generation Jacob Beam," she said, alluding to

---

3. Charles Cowdery, *Bourbon, Straight: The Uncut and Unfiltered Story of American Whiskey* (Chicago: Made and Bottled in Kentucky, 2004), 25.

4. This name was granted by a Congressional resolution in 1964.

5. Cf. "History: The Story Behind the Spirit," accessed Jun. 7, 2017, http://kybourbon-trail.com/index.php/history

the patriarch of the family.

She went on to explain how Beam, like most distilleries, was shut down in 1919 during Prohibition and was forced to liquidate its inventory. Jim Beam, great-grandson of the founder, figured this period would not last long, so he carefully studied aquifer maps for areas most rich in limestone, and eventually found a choice piece of land in Clermont, Kentucky. His wisdom paid off.

Prohibition was eventually repealed in 1933, and they started up where they had left off. The distillery has grown quite a bit since then. They now have nineteen 35,000-gallon fermenters and have produced over twelve million barrels of bourbon to date. Their White Label Jim Beam is the most recognized bourbon in the world, which might explain the enthusiasm of a Scotsman who recently toured the plant. While his countrymen might be known for producing great scotch, he was forced to admit that by coming to Jim Beam, he had arrived at "the Mecca."

The dynasty of Beam distillers and their artistry have shaped the industry so much, they could very well be considered the American aristocracy in the bourbon industry. I found this out firsthand at the end of my tour when Erica made a passing reference to their current Master Distiller, whose last name was Noe.

The Beam dynasty begun by Jacob, Miss Boone explained, was later transferred to the Noe line when T. Jeremiah Beam—great, great grandson of Jacob—did not have children. His sister Margaret married Frederick Booker Noe, and their son Frederick Booker Noe II would continue the family tradition begun centuries before. She perhaps noticed my disappointment at what appeared to be a break from tradition and candidly explained, "It's just like a king who produces no male offspring and passes on his crown to the princess."

The original Beam name, however, can still be found throughout the bourbon world. The master distiller at Heaven Hill, Kentucky's largest distillery, is cousin Parker Beam, who has been sharing his knowledge for over fifty-three years. He is joined by his son, Craig Beam, who will no doubt continue enriching the bourbon family tree.

"I love what I do," Erica admitted. "I am not just an employee; I am a member of the family..." Her words trailed off as she begged pardon for "getting teary-eyed." When she regained her composure, I asked, "Why the tears?"

"It's the heritage," she responded. "You have no idea what it means to be able to trace your roots back 200 years. It gives such a sense of self-awareness."

Hotbeds of Distilling Prowess

This same sense of intense pride shines through in every distillery you find in the Bluegrass State. Employees at each one, even those not directly related to patriarchal figures, pride themselves in simply being a part of this rich tradition.

It is for this reason that one should not visit the area without a stop at Buffalo Trace in Frankfort. They are the only distillery in Kentucky that continued to operate uninterrupted during Prohibition, because they were allowed to sell their product for medicinal purposes. No longer being limited to curing the body, they are now permitted to delight the souls of bourbon connoisseurs the world over. Their finest product, George T. Stagg, even won the International Spirit of the World Award one year by knocking off the always favored Highland Park 18 Scotch Whiskey from the Northern Highlands.

"Spirits are continually getting better and more sophisticated each year," says noted spirits reviewer Paul Pacult. "It's no surprise to us that three of the top five spirits in the world hail from Kentucky, which right now is one of the hotbeds of distilling prowess."[6]

"What We Could Enjoy Every Day"

Freddie Johnson is likely one of the more knowledgeable persons in the state on bourbon and was my tour guide for the day. He said, with about as much pride as Miss Boone, that he is a third-generation employee for the distillery and described the charming way he ended up there. He was in the middle of a successful career as a network engineer, and at one point enjoyed security clearance for tracking Air Force One. He would eventually put all this aside to fulfill a twofold request of his father, Jimmy.

"He made me promise to allow him to die in his own bed," he explained, "rather than a nursing home." The other request had to do with keeping the family tradition. "He wanted me to work at Buffalo

---

6. "George T. Stagg Named Top Spirit in the World for a Second Year in a Row!" accessed Jun. 7, 2017, http://www.prnewswire.com/news-releases/george-t-stagg-named-top-spirit-in-the-world-for-second-year-in-a-row-155340915.html.

Trace while he was still alive."

Tears rolled down his cheeks as he described the day his father called with the news that both he and Freddie's brother had come down with terminal cancer and were nearing the end of their lives. Freddie did not hesitate to fulfill both of his father's wishes. He took an early retirement, returned to Kentucky, and described how he and his father took one last walk through the distillery's main warehouse on his father's ninety-second birthday. "He told me things about the distillery that his father had taught him," Freddie explained.

He then recounted the most memorable conversation he had ever had with his father while sipping from an old bottle of bourbon that had been signed by the current and previous Buffalo Trace Master Distillers.[7]

Freddie opened it to celebrate his father's ninety-fourth birthday. After pouring a shot for his father, his brother, and himself, Freddie put the cork back in the bottle.

"What on earth are you doing, son?" his father sternly asked. "There will always be old bottles of bourbon. They are being made every day, but friends and family will not always be around, and that is what bourbon is made for. Don't ever do that again."

The message was clear, he said, bourbon is meant to be enjoyed with the moment. It was the first time that his father, brother, and he had really talked since they were very young. Three hours later, Freddie helped his ailing but now delighted father into bed.

"This is the best birthday I ever had," he told his son. Eleven months later, his father and brother were both dead, but the memory of that day and the lesson learned lives on.

"There is a saying," Freddie concluded. "'If time was not a factor in our lives, this is what we could enjoy every day.'"

Made in America

Before leaving the state, I stopped at Wild Turkey distillery, took the tour, and sampled some of their excellent product. In the gift shop, I had a chat with Scott and Beth Ryan, who had come from Columbus, Ohio. Mr. Ryan explained how they had decided to travel Kentucky's Bourbon Trail because he had seen an episode of John Ratzenberger's

---

7. This was special because Buffalo Trace is the only distillery that has three living Master Distillers. The oldest at the time, Elmer T. Lee, was ninety-three years old and was one of only three living Master Distillers to have a bourbon named after them.

Made in America, which highlighted the bourbon-making process at Maker's Mark.

After having seen it with her own eyes, Beth described how she was attracted by the regionalism expressed along the entire Bourbon Trail. She quickly added how she was fed up with the standardization in our country.

The most meaningful part of the tour was the hands-on approach they found at Makers Mark: "Dipping your finger in a massive pot of whiskey to taste the product and then dipping your own bottle into the red wax to make your very own Maker's Mark trademark seal ... I just like the uniqueness and pride of the Kentucky bourbon industry," she said.

As I left the state of Kentucky, I was happy for having traveled the Bourbon Trail, and I agree with the Ryans. This detour allowed me to discover yet one more example of American regionalism. However, I was only able to see it because I went *off the beaten path*.

Cheese Artisans and American Somewhereness

BY NORMAN FULKERSON

The backlash against standardization can be seen in the refreshing and explosive interest in artisan cheeses. The movement came about organically as American cheese artisans began experimenting with local products interacting with the terroir, or the taste of the place. The result has been prize-winning cheese from American producers that show organic solutions have a future.

For some time now, American "artisans," as they are called, have been producing world-class cheeses that rival those of France, and by doing so, they prove that Kraft is not the only game in town.

Cheese History

A cheese *artisan* is someone who uses distinctive or original recipes to make cheese in small batches by hand. They are comparable to those who might produce a piece of furniture or clothing that has a unique design. Their artistry is similar to bees who extract the sweet nectar from local flowers to produce honey that is particular to a given area.

In the case of American cheesemakers, their creativity results in a product that is refreshingly homemade and is the fruit of a tradition that dates back to the early seventeenth century. It was then that farms on the East Coast, most especially New England, began making cheese. It had been a predominantly at-home or on-the-farm industry because the milk had to be consumed quickly or processed in other ways. The cream that floated to the top was used for butter, leaving what was left—skimmed milk—for making cheese.

Until the early 1800s, there was no such thing as a cheese factory because there was simply no need for one. With the influx of European immigrants and the sudden growth of America, all that changed. Civilization and the cheese-making craft eventually moved west towards the Great Lakes, and what had started out small would become quite a large industry.

Cheese factories, often family-operated, began popping up all over

Wisconsin where the cow population kept pace with the human one. It was not long until the railroads reached this region, and along with them came a greater demand for cheese. In the latter part of the nineteenth century, cheese factories continued to multiply across southern Wisconsin and northern Illinois.

In 1903, a Canadian-born businessman named James L. Kraft started a wholesale cheese business in Chicago. After a bumpy start, the company would go on to develop thirty-one varieties by 1914. Two years later, Kraft invented a way to pasteurize cheese that eliminated the need for refrigeration. He was granted a patent for a product that came to be known as "processed cheese."

What most people do not know is that while some companies were sacrificing quality for quantity, others were not.

Cheese Artisans of America

Ignazio "Ig" Vella was only three and a half when his father, Gaetano "Tom" Vella, opened Vella Cheese Company in 1931. He vividly remembers the trips to San Francisco with his father to help throw the cheese wheels out the back of the family's truck.

Both Tom and his young son personally knew J.L. Kraft who, at that time, was using a horse and buggy to distribute cheese. Mr. Vella points out that "a lot of people started trying to make cheese, but got out of the business because they realized it was spelled W-O-R-K."

"There are still people trying to cut corners," he continued, "especially on the raw milk cheese varieties." Mr. Vella does not cut corners, and his attention to detail has paid off. He remembered very vividly when he made his first Asiago, a cheese named after the town near Venice. An Italian couple came into his store and sampled a bit. "This is better Asiago than we get back home in Italy," they both commented.

Visitors from Toma, Italy, had the same surprise when they entered the store and sampled Mr. Vella's Toma cow's milk cheese, originally developed in their region of Italy. Overcome by the taste of the American version, they exclaimed, "*Molto buono, molto buono!* (Very good!)"

While European visitors rave over what they discover in America, Mr. Vella is not surprised.

"We just never got the recognition for the quality of our cheeses, especially in the last 25 years—but we have always been there," he adds with emphasis.

American "Somewhereness"

The secret to great American cheeses is no secret at all. The success they enjoy comes from their ability to take advantage of the rich resources offered in their particular region. It is what author Rowan Jacobsen calls *terroir*, a French word that means "taste of place." He is the author of *American Terroir* and describes how such creativity is "anathema to a certain conservative European school of gastronomes who believe that the Land of the Golden Arches is incapable of producing foods and drinks that embody a particular 'somewhereness.'"[1] He affirms that the American version of terroir rivals that of Europe.

Al and Catherine Renzi are but one example. They started Yellow Springs Farm in Chester Springs, Pennsylvania ten years ago, and later discovered the horticultural riches of the land they owned after doing a botanical survey. This eventually led to a plant nursery and then a few goats which Mrs. Renzi defined as just a "friends-and-family thing." Over the years, they were able to get a permit from the PDA (Pennsylvania Department of Agriculture) to make and sell goat cheese. They have come a long way since then and are now members of both the American Cheese Society (ACS) founded in 1983, and the Chester County Cheese Artisans.

Their Red Leaf cheese won an ACS award in 2010 while their Nutcracker took first place. Red Leaf is wrapped in sycamore leaves that grow on their property. Both kinds of cheese, she says, are examples of their intent to integrate the horticultural plant richness of the landscape with the cheese.

The interest in local food in America, she went on to explain, is encouraging people to understand that, just as the French have their great cheeses, so does America.

"They are as unique and varied," she continued, "as our local indigenous botanical resources, microclimates, histories, and cultures. That is the essence of why there can be a Chester County cheese artisan. We have the richness of sycamore and black walnut trees, and that's what makes our cheese special. It is what our goats eat. It's the geology of the land that produces the herbaceous layer of pasture they stand on. It's the weather, the climate, the air."

There is a long history of what she defines as a "dairy heritage" in

---

1. Rowan Jacobsen, *American Terroir: Savoring the Flavor of our Woods, Waters, and Fields*, (New York, Bloomsbury USA, 2010), 2-3.

this area, and it embraces everything from Breyer's ice cream to Philadelphia cream cheese.

"France Is in Trouble"

The Renzis went to Italy and met with a lot of cheesemakers who were more than willing to share their recipes. However, they were told that a recipe alone is not what makes good cheese. "Your cheese will never turn out like ours," the Italians said, "because you have different goats which eat different foods. You have a different climate, air, water. You are different. Your essence of being is different." In the final analysis, the Renzis were told to go home and "make your own cheese."

Fifty percent of what one tastes in cheese comes from *affinage*, or the aging process.

In this way, the Americans learned more than the art of making good cheese and acquired a valuable lesson in organic society which respects regional differences. This is excellent news for cheese lovers since France, always known for its great cheeses, is actually in decline. Mr. Jacobsen attributes this to the eating habits of the newer generations, which are changing. "French consumers," he says, "are going to the supermarket."[2]

American cheesemaker Mateo Kehler found this out firsthand when he last visited France. He and his brother Andy are producing world-class cheese at their Jasper Hill Farm in Greensboro, Vermont. He spoke with French cheesemaker Hervé Mons, who affirmed that terroir in France "has been defined" and is actually in decline.

During that trip, Mr. Kehler presented his Winnimere cheese to a top French *affineur* to get his opinion. An *affineur* is a person who oversees the *affinage* or "aging process" of cheese making. Fifty percent of what one tastes in the final product is the result of proper aging. It is for this reason that cheesemakers will often send their cheeses to the

---

2. Ibid., 233.

best *affineurs*, even if it means sending their cheese to the other side of the country.

After taking one taste of Jasper Farms' products, the French *affineur* was forced to admit, "No such cheese has been made in France for thirty years." Mr. Kehler presented the same cheese to a French consul-general—the man charged with furthering French culture abroad. The stunned Frenchman tasted the cheese, looked up and said, "France is in trouble."[3]

Capturing the Gold

Jasper Farms is not the only cheesemaker turning heads abroad. Rebecca Sherman Orozco is the communications director for the American Cheese Society, and told me about the World Championship Cheese Contest held every two years.

"Overall, U.S. cheesemakers dominated the competition," she said, "earning gold medals in 46 of the total 77 categories judged." Wisconsin dominated with twenty-one gold medals. One of them went to Carr Valley Cheese in La Valle, Wisconsin, which is one of the oldest producers in America.

You may not have heard of it, but Carr Valley has been around since 1902 and therefore predates Kraft. Its website describes the producer's "passion for cheesemaking excellence" that runs deep. Today, fourth-generation owner Sid Cook is one of a small handful of certified American master cheesemakers. This distinction is only awarded to veteran Wisconsin craftsmen who complete a rigorous fifteen-year advanced training and education program.[4]

At the 2012 World Cheese Awards held in the United Kingdom, Jasper Hill captured the gold for its Harbison cheese, against over 2,300 other cheeses from around the world.

Great cheesemakers have always existed in America. They are proof that within a land that appears to offer only universal sameness, one finds wonderful examples of American somewhereness. This is yet another marvelous example of the regionalism that can be found when one wanders *off the beaten path*.

---

3. Jacobsen, *American Terroir*, 233.

4. http://www.carrvalleycheese.com

CHAPTER 18

Culture Is in the Grits

BY JOHN HORVAT II

Organic solutions do not have to be sophisticated like bourbon or artisan cheeses. They can be found in some of the simplest things in life. The example of grits is perfect since it is something accessible to so many, especially in the South, where grit corn grows well. However, the variables that influence the simple ingredients in grits make it a true expression of a culture.

"**M**odern culture is defined by this extraordinary freedom to ransack the world storehouse and to engorge any and every style it comes upon," writes Daniel Bell in his book *The Cultural Contradictions of Capitalism.* This notion of culture is defined by the individual's claimed right to experience everything in the name of self-fulfillment. It is a quest Bell describes thus: "[N]othing is forbidden, all is to be explored."

This eclectic notion of culture is incredibly superficial and individualistic, cold and artificial. It fails to make those rich connections within a society, its shared attitudes, values, products, and practices. Like so many words in our society today, culture becomes whatever the individual wants it to be.

There are those who think culture is about surrounding yourself with certified "organic" foods, craft beers, and free-range chickens. While such things do have organic aspects, there is something terribly inorganic, uncultural, and expensive about this perspective.

That is because the proper use of the term "organic" presupposes a society. Inorganic things are mechanical, mass-produced, and indifferent to place. Truly organic things spring from life and come from the natural interaction of people, places, and things. They have soul and meaning.

In an organic culture, the best things in life are simple and accessible. People take basic elements and raise them to amazing degrees of perfection. The result is an extremely rich, even sublime, expression of a people.

A good example of this is grits. You cannot get more basic than grits. Nothing could be simpler than this southern staple of ground corn boiled in salted water and milk. However, nothing can be further from the real thing than the industrialized add-water-milk-and-quick-stir varieties that pass for grits at so many diners and homes.

Authentic grits require the human element to enter into their making. People then develop local versions that give soul to the ground corn mixture.

Real organic grits are simple, but they do take time. Some say they should simmer for hours at the lowest possible temperature to get all the corn flavor into the dish. Grits can be mixed with diced bacon, bell pepper, onion, or any other often local ingredients, allowing for an enormous variety of grit dishes. Charleston's archetypal grits, for example, are served with freshly caught roe shrimp.

That is the beauty of organic society: No two grits are alike. There is no one-grit-fits-all dish. The key ingredients are all the same, but the embellishments are so refreshingly different and local.

That is why you cannot just buy "organic society" grits off a Whole Foods shelf. There must be that vital connection between the product and the consumer. True grits need to be anchored in a place and loved by inhabitants.

Indeed, there was a time when people could perceive where they were simply by the flavor of the local grits. Each small town or region in the South has its own variety of grit corn that came from seeds handed down over generations. "They all have a voice," observes Charleston chef Shawn Brock in a *Wall Street Journal* interview. "Each one carries stories, each has its own personality, each is a history lesson."

Such varieties of corn are generally not as commercially viable because they do not produce huge yields, but their incredible taste makes up for any shortcomings. Locals become sensitive to such tastes and naturally prefer them over others.

Not only does the variety of corn make a difference to grits, but the actual soil where the corn is grown also influences the taste. Corn, like so many products, picks up the flavor of the land where it grows. Grits connoisseurs can detect the subtle difference between corn from bottom land and that from mountainside plots. Climate also enters into the equation, making grits part of Southern culture, since grit corn does not do well in harsh, northern climes.

When people, grits, and place organically come together, something amazing happens. By constantly adjusting available materials to local tastes, the producer and consumer become the "co-creators" of these dishes. A local cuisine develops when chefs and those who cook constantly adjust local dishes and native ingredients to reflect what local people like. They experience the spiritual joy of tasting the product of their joint creativity with the materials at hand.

That is why true grits belong to everyone in the region, not just one social group. Excellent variations are served in fine restaurants, family homes, and rustic truck stops. Simple grits become a point of unity and a true expression of a people and place.

When people share not only grits, but all sorts of foods, fashions, and styles, a rich culture is born. Everything becomes a manifestation of the strong personality of those who inhabit a region. People come to understand that their region is made for them and they for their region, which offers them a wide variety of supreme delights no other place can offer.

"In a highly developed culture, this sense of style permeates everything," writes Richard Weaver. "It is in dress and manners, in art and institutions, in architecture and cookery. It imparts tone to the whole of society by keeping before its members the standard of the right and not right."

That is the problem with much of our modern "culture." It isn't culture. Postmodern "culture" is about disconnected experiences that have no meaning, narrative, or context. There is no organic relationship between the cultural object, the people, and place. A dreary sameness has descended upon society. The globalized commercialization of everything tends to reduce real culture into "a handful of quaint old customs, maintained like bones in a museum."

Thus "culture" comes to mean the top-down production of exotic (and expensive) foods and handcrafted products available globally. Some think it "cultural" to adopt modern architectural styles indifferent to the climate and place. Others seek to find "culture" in natural water from Iceland, tasty mushrooms from Transylvania, or any other such products that may be excellent in quality, but that have nothing to do with the locality. The vital link has been severed.

There is nothing wrong with occasionally experiencing the culture of others. It is wrong to assume, however, that you must constantly look outward to acquire culture. You must, above all, look inward and to your origins. Whether it be a local clam chowder or gumbo, a cowboy boot, or a region's distinctive musical tradition, everyone can claim to be the part of some culture. Culture is not found in some prepackaged experience. Sometimes it is found in the grits.

"The Ham Lady" and the Art of Ham Curing

BY NORMAN FULKERSON

Key to the whole idea of organic solutions are those people and families who take the simple things and develop a passion for excellence that makes the product a real masterpiece. This is often something that is developed over generations and highlights the importance of family and tradition. It also creates a process that is full of passion and poetry strongly rooted in the land and culture of a people.

Spain is a country that is world-renowned for its pork products. Everything from air-dried cured ham to their mouth-watering *Jamón Serrano* has delighted travelers for ages. One need not travel to the Iberian Peninsula, however, to enjoy such culinary masterpieces. The age-old and time-tested art of ham curing is alive and well, but can only be found if you get off the beaten path in Princeton, Kentucky.

A Family Recipe Discovered in a Seventeenth Century Will

This tiny town in the western part of the Blue Grass State is most commonly known for a little country shop called Col. Bill Newsom's Old Mill Store. It was originally called H.C. Newsom's Store in 1917, the year Col. Newsom's grandfather Hosea first opened its doors to the public.

It was the typical country grocery store that carried everything from broomsticks and glassware to pickles... and of course, crackers in barrels. At that time, however, aged hams were not part of their inventory because most people cured their own at home. With changing times and a faster pace of life, the family custom of ham curing fell by the wayside. This was not the case with Hosea, who clung to the tradition passed on to him by his ancestors, namely William Newsom, who first came to America from Newsham Hall, England in 1642.

Hosea passed away in 1933 and left the store and the accumulated wisdom of ham curing to his son, Bill Newsom. The young lad cultivated an interest in preserving this lost art. One can only imagine his enthusiasm when he fortuitously uncovered the seventeenth century ancestral will of William Newsom with the family recipe for ham curing. Bill Newsom, who later became a Kentucky Colonel, incorporated the wisdom of the past with what he had learned through his father by word of mouth. This invaluable knowledge was slowly imbibed by his daughter Nancy, who would go on to take over the family business in 1987.

Nancy Newsom, affectionately known as "the Ham Lady." Staying true to family tradition and a family recipe going back centuries, her Kentucky aged hams have become world-renowned.

The quality of her products has earned her the moniker "The Ham Lady" by *The Wall Street Journal*, which has featured her in several articles.

The secret to the mouth-watering ham produced by Newsom's is a three-step process and a certain innate sense that goes into each one.

Ham Curing Process

It all begins with the hand-rubbing of a salt and brown sugar mix deep into the meat. This old-fashioned method requires repeated rubs allowing this mixture to eventually seep through to the bone. There are absolutely no nitrates used, however, and this is one of the main differences between a Newsom Ham and the mass-produced, store-bought versions.

Besides killing unwanted bacteria, nitrates give ham that healthy, even if a bit artificial, red color. Newsom hams, on the contrary, acquire their deep, rich wine color through a natural aging process while the salt kills any unhealthy organisms.

Once the meat has absorbed these two ingredients, each ham is hand-washed and placed in the smokehouse, but only after the skin is just right: not too dry but, more importantly, not too moist. This is decided by "the touch" of "the Ham Lady." This touch, she explains, was not something she was taught, but is rather the decades-long experience of working in a smokehouse since she was just a little girl.

The hams only begin to be slow or "cold smoked" when spring's warmth sets in. That is when Mrs. Newsom starts a fire in an iron kettle, with a mixture of hickory wood and sawdust.

"Before I Die, I am Going to Make a Pilgrimage to Princeton"

Then comes the most important part of the ham curing process: the July sweats. The humid Kentucky summers produce an assortment of mold on the outer edge of the ham, giving the final product its unique flavor, much like a good cheese.

Smokehouses are different, Mrs. Newsom kindly explained, and they have two. The older one, she affirms, has a better mold which gives the meat more personality. She knows this by a sense of taste equal to that of her sense of touch.

Since Newsom's does not use climate control—as do large producers—their hams are partially subjected to fluctuating weather conditions that only improve the final product. During particularly wet days, the ham takes on moisture and expands into the outer mold-covered skin. During dryer periods, it contracts and brings with it accumulated flavors.

This process is similar to Kentucky Bourbon. The moonshine that originally goes into virgin white oak barrels takes on a marvelous amber color and wood-tinged flavor through the expanding and extracting that takes place during the change of seasons.

The Newsoms understand, as do bourbon producers, that excellence takes time. It is for this reason that Nancy, just as her ancestors before her, is not in a rush. They won't sell a ham that is not aged for at least ten months, whereas some will continue perfecting for twenty-two.

Staying true to tradition has earned Newsom's faithful customers like Randy Oehmig from faraway Crystal River, Florida. In the early sixties, his father went on a "ham hunt...searching the nation for the best salt-cured country ham." His quest for the holy grail of ham led him to Col. Bill Newsom. The Oehmigs have been serving Newsom hams at holiday meals ever since. Mr. Oehmig, at seventy years of age, describes them as "one of the finest things I've ever laid on my tongue. The combination of the smoky flavor and saltiness is almost indescribable."[1] During a phone interview, he said he has three of her hams in his cooler. One of them is four years old. His devotion to her is such that he swears, "Before I die, I am going to make a pilgrimage to Princeton."

---

1. Stuart Englert, "Smokehouses: Preserving Food and Tradition," Nov. 2, 2013, accessed Jun. 7, 2017, http://americanprofile.com/articles/smokehouses-preserving-food-and-tradition-video.

Glowing Accolades from Coast to Coast

They are not alone in their praise. Staying true to the family tradition, Nancy Newsom has earned a reputation among connoisseurs, and acclaim in restaurants from California to New York. She has been featured in numerous journals like *Gourmet*, *Southern Living*, and *Esquire*. *New York Magazine* had a 2005 article[2] about the restaurant Egg which had just opened in Brooklyn. They declared Nancy's ham the "undisputed star" and "undersung American treasure," whereas Jonathan Gold with the *LA Weekly* dubbed them "astonishing."[3]

One of her most prized endorsements came from Peter Kaminsky, cook, author, and renowned barbeque chef. He is considered by some to be a specialist in all things pork which has earned him the nickname

Newsom's hams have received accolades from coast to coast, but one of its most prized honors is to be the only American ham in the Museo del Jamon, in Aracena, Spain.

"hamthrologist." He has tasted hams from all over the world, but the most glowing accolades in his book, *PigPerfect*,[4] are served up for Nancy Newsom.

He gave further testimony to the quality of her product during a blindfolded taste test at a Fancy Food Show in New York City's Jacob Javits Convention Center. This event was put on by David Arnold, founder of the Museum of Food and Drink.[5] The purpose of the tasting was not so much to rank the ham, as it was to see if "American hams could stand up to their European cousins."[6] Mr. Kaminsky was given thirteen hams to sample and immediately picked Nancy's as the undisputed best.

2. http://nymag.com/nymetro/food/openings/12385/.

3. Jonathan Gold, "Going Ham for the Holidays," *LA Weekly*, Dec. 9, 2009, accessed Jun. 7, 2017, http://www.laweekly.com/restaurants/going-ham-for-the-holidays-2162853.

4. Peter Kaminsky, *Pig Perfect* (New York: Hyperion, 2005).

5. http://www.mofad.org/.

6. "Ham List," accessed Jun. 7, 2017, http://www.aamp.com/news/documents/RawTalentHamBooklet.pdf.

Only American Ham in Spain's Museo del Jamón

Peter Kaminsky happened to be with "the Ham Lady" when she was given the greatest honor an American ham producer could ever dream of receiving. In May of 2009, Nancy Newsom was invited to participate in the Fifth World Congress of Dry Cured Hams in Aracena, Spain. Just to be invited was an honor in itself when one considers how Spain is known for having the best hams in the world. "The Ham Lady" was utterly astounded when one of her two-year-old hams was given a place of honor in the *Museo del Jamón* in Aracena, Spain. It was the only ham in the United States of America to be "invited" much less kept for ham lovers across the world to admire.

Through it all, Nancy remains humble with all the attention and continues to relish the fact that she is preserving a "lost art." She is also content to be just "the Ham Lady" from Princeton.

"As the daughter of a man who was quite 'homespun' himself," she writes on her website, "I tend to hold to the methods of our forefathers, folklore and history itself."[7] She sees the yearly ham curing process as "a reenactment of a historical tradition" and is perfectly at ease with the limited number of hams she can produce.

If you call to place an order, you will not get an answering machine—so common in our mechanized world. The phone might even ring off the hook, but there will always be a human being to answer. More often than not, the reward for patience will be the lilting Southern accent of Nancy Newsom herself. She won't rush you off the phone either, because customer service brings her joy as does her time writing poetry down by "the cove."

An especially interesting composition, "Gnarled Trees Are the Best," reads like a self-portrait of the Newsom family. She describes such knotty specimens, which defy the test of time, as feats of nature.

"No matter the storms and gales of life . . ." she writes, "the old trees roots are deep"; and so it is with the remarkable history of Newsom hams. To find them, one only needs to get *off the beaten path* ... and look for the gnarled tree. Or you can call and speak personally to "the Ham Lady" from Princeton.

---

7. Accessed Jun. 7, 2017, http://www.newsomscountryham.com/losartourtra.html.

CHAPTER 20

Mammy's: The Real Cracker Barrel

BY NORMAN FULKERSON

The term "organic" comes from society's resemblance to a living organism. Organic society respects and allows each person's unique individuality to develop naturally, in opposition to the mechanistic and socialistic society which imposes a suffocating standardization. Refreshing examples of determined people finding unique solutions can be found everywhere, especially if one travels off the beaten path.

In an ever-changing world, one thing seems to always remain the same: a meal at Cracker Barrel Old Country Store. It is perhaps that universal sameness, both in food and décor, which always leaves me a bit disappointed. While the artifacts that hang on the walls are authentic, they have nothing to do with the owner, nor those serving the food.

This fabricated ambience made up of assorted farm tools, metal signs, family photographs, cast-iron cookware, and old-fashioned toys might have an initial appeal, but it falls short of satisfying a deeper desire for something authentically down-home. It lacks the individuality we so appreciate, and merely delivers an ambience that is mass produced in cookie-cutter fashion coast to coast.

What we desire in a place that calls itself an Old Country Store is organic. This is exactly what I found *off the beaten path* at Mammy's restaurant in Bardstown, Kentucky.

Hourigan Family Recipe Book

As with other examples of organic society in America, I was not looking for such a place when I drove into Bardstown on a particularly nice, sunny fall morning. This charming city earned the Rand McNally distinction of being the Most Beautiful Small Town in America for 2012,[1] so I figured it might be a good place to find an authentically down-home breakfast rather than the standardized version so commonly dished out at Cracker Barrel.

This is what led me to Mammy's and a memorable conversation

---

1. Accessed Jun. 7, 2017, http://www.bestoftheroad.com/botr.php/town/bardstown-ky/6234.

Christy Clark proudly holding the Hourigan Family Recipe Book which she inherited from her grandmother.

with owner Christy Clark, who took time from her busy schedule to tell me the history of her restaurant.

What really got my attention was the fact that all the food she serves is prepared with recipes taken from the book she inherited from her grandmother Hourigan.

"Woodya like to see it," she asked. She quickly disappeared into the back room and returned with the *Hourigan Family Recipe Book*. As I thumbed through it, I could not help but chuckle at the food stains visible on some pages. They were signs of special moments in the kitchen, and Christy's appreciation for it revealed a key to her success.

Antique Café

Since she was a small girl, Christy had always been interested in cooking. She was often seen hanging around the stove, and remembers the aromas wafting through the air where she grew up in Gravel Switch, Kentucky. More importantly, she recalls the happiness such culinary scents produced on the faces of grandkids and farm workers.

It seemed reasonable, therefore, that she would one day open a restaurant. That is not what she and her mother Thelma had in mind, however, when they first went into business together with Christy's Collections, her antique shop, and Sew It Seams by Thelma.

Her mother occupied the back room while she took the front in a little shop on Main Street. She quickly filled it with antique items while her mother grew a clientele with her sewing skills. With the growth of their original business ventures, they became very busy, but never lost their appreciation for good home cooking and the desire to share it with others.

"We were always a wantin' something to eat," Christy said, "and were just dying for some pinto beans and cornbread." So they decided to satisfy this craving by opening an antique café and decided to call it Mammy's after her grandmother Hourigan. After a trip to the grocery store, they excitedly began cooking, though the opening day turned out to be dismal.

"We had all the food prepared, but no one showed up," she explained with a laugh. They solved the problem as Southerners do: Christy went out into the street and literally grabbed the first person who happened to be walking by.

"Come on in," she said to the stunned local. "We're a-cookin'! Try our food." That man was Guffy Wilson. He found it hard to say no to this excited group of Southern ladies who merely wanted someone to enjoy their food, and for whom the check was secondary. They huddled around him as he ate lunch and with each bite kept asking, "Do you like it?"

Mr. Wilson liked it so much he became a regular, and through word of mouth, others followed.

Birth of Mammy's

As the numbers increased, so did the need for proper seating. They simply had no place to put customers. Some sat on the antique bed from Christy's Collections; others found chairs next to her mother's upholstering table.

"We were clueless as to what we were doing," Christy explained. "We just wanted to make people happy and to feel comfortable and relaxed." Without realizing it, she was pointing out a fundamental characteristic of organic society. Such places are not bureaucratically planned in a sterile way, but rather spring up spontaneously from one's good impulses.

It might have been organic, but there were rough spots that still needed to be ironed out. Without proper ventilation, for example, they were forced to keep the back door open. While the locals didn't seem to mind going back to work smelling like a piece of bacon, Christy explained, members of the health department did.

"We love what you are doing," they said, "but you can't do this." They were forced to move into the vacant building next door, and thus Mammy's was born. What started as an antique shop and blossomed into a café eventually turned into a full-fledged restaurant.

They now have thirty-five regulars who call Mammy's home when they are hungry for a good meal and Southern hospitality. More importantly, they are attracting tourists willing to bypass the local Cracker Barrel in favor of a more authentic version of down-home America.

Clara Bell

Authenticity is perhaps the key ingredient to her success. Everything in the restaurant has a story, even Clara Bell, the life-size Holstein cow that has a prominent place in the front window. Christy found her one day while on a shopping spree just sitting in a store window. To her delight, the owner was trying to get rid of her. Christy jumped at the opportunity.

As a child growing up on a farm, they always named their milk cows, so Christy decided to have a contest to name her new Holstein, with the winner receiving a $50 gift certificate. They wound up receiving over three hundred entries. After going through all the names, Clara Bell won and has since become a central figure and point of reference for those driving down the street.

This is but one example of how Mammy's makes a person feel they are part of the family.

Memory Walls

"I just want people to feel like they are at Grandma's house," Christy explained. With a one-page menu and family-like surroundings, Mammy's has what she describes as a "Waltons feel."

Besides the prominent photo of Grandmother Hourigan hanging on the wall as you enter, there is also a picture of the Breakfast Club, whose members make up "the regulars." There is a special place for what could be considered their founding member, the late Judge Bob Heaton. He passed away in July of 2012, but enjoyed eating at Mammy's for five years.

These are not just wall ornaments. They make up part of what Christy calls her Memory Walls because they remind her of the people she does not want to forget.

One of Mammy's favorites was John Pruitt. Like other Breakfast Club members, he appreciated the dollar cup of coffee, but he received a treatment one rarely finds away from home. Mr. Pruitt was a 93-year-old diabetic, and Christy adapted the menu to his diet with sugar-free jellies and desserts, or an extra piece of sausage if he so desired.

"Anything he asked for," she says, "he got."

Such bending to the needs of the customer might seem out of the ordinary, but this is something else which sets Mammy's apart from others. It is something the casual outsider who stops off for a meal will never know.

Those Undergoing Chemo Eat for Free

In January of 2009, Christy's mother was diagnosed with cancer and had to undergo surgery and several painful rounds of chemotherapy. While the surgery was successful, she had a relapse and eventually succumbed to the illness.

Christy never forgot the discomfort the chemo caused her mother, and made the decision to do the only thing she could to alleviate the pain of anyone going through a similar ordeal. Thus was born a custom one would not expect to find in a modern-day eatery: "If you are undergoing chemo treatment," she explained choking back tears, "but are able to get up and come in, you will eat at Mammy's for free."

Dan Bennett, who can be seen in his picture on the Memory Wall smiling from ear to ear with Christy and her daughter Robin, was one such patient. He came in every morning for a year to eat his favorite, French toast. When he was too sick to come in, Christy modified her original offer. For Dan and another patient who were simply too sick to come into the restaurant, she, like the doctors of old, made house calls and delivered the meal of choice to them.

Dan eventually died of cancer, but described the compassion he received at Mammy's as "life changing." Chemo may not have been able to save his life, but Mammy's good food and affection breathed new life into his soul.

Mammy's food just might have been a contributing factor of not only healing the soul of Kelly Clark, but her body as well. She is Christy's husband's niece. After giving birth to her son, Kelly was diagnosed with cancer and subsequently endured a whole year of chemotherapy. She took advantage of Christy's kindness to satisfy her craving for the only thing she could eat, grilled chicken salad. According to Christy, "She is fine as wine now."

Saving Clara Bell

So is Mammy's, but not without bumps in the road. In June 2013 a fire started in the building next door and threatened to destroy all Christy's hard work. By the time she arrived, faithful townspeople were grabbing everything they could to save it from the fire.

"Everything in the restaurant has a meaning to me," she explained, "and now it was about to go up in smoke."

When the firemen arrived, their primary concern was extinguishing the flames. They were shocked by the insistence of Mammy's customers to save the memorabilia they had grown to love, most notably Clara Bell. Christy laments not having a photo of the firemen hauling the giant Holstein cow through the smoke and safely out the front door as the loyal customers cheered them on. "Yeah, you saved Clara Bell," they yelled. Not a single piece of the treasured items was lost in the fire.

In the weeks it took to get Mammy's up and running, Christy would have a daily cup of coffee with 93-year-old John Pruitt on the bench outside. After the restaurant re-opened, he surprised her with a collection he had taken up with all the men at the Breakfast Club table. It was a goodwill gesture to help Christy get back on her feet after the fire, and also an expression of gratitude for all she had done for him. She resisted the offer and said she did not need it. Try as she might, they would not take "no" for an answer.

"I want you to take this," Mr. Pruitt said insistently. "If I didn't have this place to go to, I probably wouldn't have much of a reason to get out of bed in the morning." Other visitors feel the same. It is for this reason that Mammy's earned 3rd Place in 2013 for the favorite non-franchise restaurant in the state by readers of *Kentucky Living* magazine.[2] Mr. Pruitt is gone now, as are Judge Heaton

Clara Bell, the life size Holstein cow, normally has a prominent place in the restaurant's front window.

and a few others whose memories remain on the walls of this restaurant that was born organically from the heart.

The reader should not interpret this article as an anti-Cracker Barrel statement. It is merely the recognition of what truly is another charming example of organic society in America. I have eaten at Cracker Barrel many times before and will do so again, but when I am in Bardstown, Kentucky, I will get *off the beaten path* and enjoy some of Mammy's home cooking.

---

2. "2013 Best in Kentucky," Apr. 1, 2013, accessed Jun. 7, 2017, https://www.kentuckyliving.com/life-in-kentucky/features-life-in-kentucky/2013-best-in-kentucky.

"The Carrot Cake Lady"– Still Making It the Way Grandma Did

BY NORMAN FULKERSON

The interesting thing about organic solutions is they work in tandem with other Return to Order principles. The organic development of a product like carrot cake can also call forth representative characters who impact the whole community. Also, traditions are born that become an essential part of the local culture. All society benefits when organic solutions enter into the economy and culture.

Like so many things in our fast-paced society, the art of cake baking in America, dating back to the 1930s, has been simplified. There still exists an appreciation for the made-from-scratch version produced with mom's tender loving hands. More often than not, however, our mother's recipes are adaptations of their mothers'. Those, in turn, are eventually bequeathed to the next generation.

A heavenly slice of Lloyd's Carrot Cake.

This is the secret to the success of Lloyd's Carrot Cake bakery in the Bronx, New York. Founded by Lloyd Adams in 1986, their desserts have become wildly successful because of a recipe for carrot cake Mr. Adams inherited from his grandmother. In a country that invented the "add water and stir" cake mixes, Lloyd's variety is a refreshing reprieve for Americans to satisfy their sweet tooth with something genuine.

Medieval Origins

Carrot cake has been around since the early nineteenth century, but its origin is often traced back to the Middle Ages. During that time, sugar and other sweeteners were hard to come by, so Europeans opted for the orange vegetable as a substitute to make carrot pudding. Someone—perhaps a grandmother—had the idea of placing the pudding into an oven. The baked product came to be known as a carrot cake.

The oldest known recipe dates back to 1892 and was found in the tiny village of Kaiseraugst in Switzerland where it was very popular, especially for children's birthday parties.[1] Baking cakes, however, would later go through profound changes.

Cooking Is "an Act of Love"

In large part, the transformation in cake baking can be attributed to Pittsburgh native John D. Duff. In 1930 he patented[2] an idea of what

"The Carrot Cake Lady," Betty Campbell Adams, owner of Lloyd's Carrot Cake bakery in the Bronx, New York, with Award.

would come to be known as "cake mix." Mr. Duff's recipe for pastry products was simple: Provide all the ingredients—flour, molasses, eggs, and such—in a dehydrated form and leave the cook with a simple task: add water, stir, and bake. American grandmas, along with their unique recipes,[3] were thus proverbially thrown under the bus.

Many women, however, rejected the novelty outright. They did so, according to psychologist Ernest Dichter, because most women saw cooking as "an act of love." The "simplicity of the mixes," he discovered, "made women feel self-indulgent. In order to enjoy the emotional rewards of presenting a homemade cake," he concluded, "they had to be persuaded that they really baked it."[4] This is likely what led Mr. Duff to modify his original patent with one that addressed the "psychological handicap involved in the use of dried or powdered eggs." He thus changed his original add-water-and-stir patent to include also "the use of fresh eggs."[5]

Capitalizing on this idea, hundreds of American companies such as

1. "The Carrot Cake," Dec, 3, 2014, accessed Jun. 7, 2017, https://thefrenchfancy.wordpress.com/2014/12/03/the-carrot-cake/.

2. Patent no. 1931892.

3. Cf. Nelson Ribeiro Fragelli, "Well-prepared dishes, A Recipe for Charity," Jul. 26, 2010, accessed Jun. 7, 2017, http://www.tfp.org/well-prepared-dishes-a-recipe-for-charity/ .

4. Michael L. Goodman, Aisha S. Dickerson, Roberta B. Ness, *Creativity in the Sciences: A Workbook Companion to Innovation Generation* (Oxford: Oxford University Press, 2013), 189.

5. Patent no. 2,016,320.

Pillsbury, General Mills, and Duncan Hines began producing "cake mixes." Betty Crocker paid heed to Dr. Dichter's discovery and gave women the sense of satisfaction they desired by allowing them to add fresh eggs to the water. "Those eggs keep it moist and tender to the last crumb," said one suggestive commercial of the 1950s, "not that you'll ever have any crumbs!"[6]

Since then, box mixes, with and without real eggs, became ubiquitous in supermarkets nationwide, and restaurants frequently serve such varieties to their patrons. All the while, Americans were left to imagine what Grandma might serve. Lloyd Adams never had that problem. He savored his grandmother's cake—the carrot version—as a boy, and with a good idea, he has earned fans around the world.

Cultivating a Tradition

Lloyd Adams was a social worker before he began baking in his Harlem apartment in the early 1980s. True to tradition and the harmonious continuation of the past, he tweaked his grandmother's carrot cake recipe until he got it the way he wanted it. At that time he was a one-man show, selling his cake to coffee shops, a loyal fan base, and a dozen wholesale customers.[7]

Lloyd Adams, founder of Lloyd's Carrot Cake Bakery.

When he told his future bride, Betty Campbell, that he wanted to be a baker, she recoiled. It did not seem a profitable way to make a living and support a family. His business strategy, however, was simple: "You have to get them to taste it. Once they taste it, we're in [business]."[8]

They eventually married and opened a small kitchen in the basement

---

6. Michael Y. Park, "A History of the Cake Mix, An Invention That Redefined 'Baking,'" *Bon Apetit*, Sept. 26, 2013, accessed Jun. 7, 2017, http://www.bonappetit.com/entertaining-style/pop-culture/article/cake-mix-history.

7. Jennifer Bleyermay, "At the Sign of the Smiling Carrot, Grief, Then Sweet Relief," *The New York Times*, May 13, 2007.

8. "Lloyd's Carrot Cake," accessed Jun. 7, 2017, http://placestogoinnewyork.com/places/1673861-Lloyd-s-Carrot-Cake/.

of her father's East Harlem apartment, but quickly outgrew it. In April 1986, they opened their first shop in the Riverdale section of the Bronx. It wasn't long before they had a faithful clientele. Their menu would later include such delicacies as pies, muffins, and red velvet cake. It was the otherworldly carrot cake, however, which kept customers coming back in droves. Lines have been known to stretch for a city block, and if you are going to stop by for Thanksgiving dessert, it might take three hours to be served.

"The Carrot Cake Lady"

In February 2007, Lloyd died suddenly of a heart attack. Hundreds attended his funeral and praised his contribution to their community. For six weeks the Riverdale store remained closed, leaving mournful customers to fear it would not reopen. One patron, from faraway Florida, left a note on the shuttered doors expressing his disappointment.

Much to her patron's relief, the bakery did not close; they were merely renovating. Mrs. Adams was determined not to let her husband's dream die with him. Six weeks later, the bakery was reopened and began churning out "70 cakes a day, using over 600 pounds of carrots and 200 pounds of cream cheese for the frosting."[9] These ingredients are the secret to Lloyd's success. Their specialty cake is not just carrot in name only. Copious amounts of the vegetable go into each one, and the mouthwatering icing is made with real cream cheese, not a hydrated variant.

Since then Mrs. Adams, who eventually earned the moniker "The Carrot Cake Lady," has opened up a new location in East Harlem that serves over 400 cakes a week. One can only imagine her surprise to find out that one of them found its way to a soldier stationed in Iraq, courtesy of his friends in the New York City Fire Department. On another occasion, a visitor from the Philippines carried one home to her mother. This led Mrs. Adams to consider putting up a map to chart the distant journeys her cakes have made, a good idea when one considers her husband's culinary masterpiece has made its ways to China, Ecuador, Israel, London, Nigeria, and eventually Costa Rica, where "The Carrot Cake Lady" was born.[10]

---

9. Bleyermay, "The Smiling Carrot," *New York Times*, May 13, 2007.

10. Winnie Hu, "A Tiny Bronx Bakery Churns Out Carrot Cakes That Travel the World," *The New York Times,* Apr. 10, 2016, accessed Jun. 7, 2017, https://www.nytimes.com/2016/04/10/nyregion/a-tiny-bronx-bakery-churns-out-carrot-cakes-that-travel-the-world.html?_r=0.

Fans of Lloyd's can take consolation in the fact that the dream started by Mr. Adams and kept alive by "The Carrot Cake Lady" will continue. Their daughter, Lilka, uses her marketing skills to run the bakery's social media operations, while son Brandon is currently the store's general manager.

"Changing the World"

In our industrialized world that has affected everything, including cake baking, one cannot help but breathe a sigh of relief to know there is an alternative to Betty Crocker. Thanks to a New Yorker who felt his recipe could make it big, Americans can enjoy a handcrafted version right at home.

Lloyd's Carrot Cake bakery in the Riverdale section of the Bronx.

"I've always had the social science view that I could change the world," Mr. Adams once said. He admitted the joy it brings "to walk into a restaurant where a customer is eating a slice of cake and hear, 'Wow, who made this carrot cake?'"[11] He might not have changed the world, but his cakes have most certainly traveled a good part of it. In a country commonly known for "cake mix," the popularity of Lloyd's made–from-scratch creations, both here and abroad, is but one more example of a paradox that exists only in America.

---

11. Accessed Jun. 7, 2017, http://www.lloydscarrotcake.com/?page_id=31.

Christmas Outside the Box

BY JOHN HORVAT II

Technology is made to serve us; we are not made to serve technology. So often, marketers seek to create an effortless world where every material comfort is maximized and every spiritual desire is minimized. The technocrats fail to realize that sometimes people need to express themselves with efforts that allow them to add a personal touch. A hyper-standardized world creates hyper-standardized experiences. What is needed is a return to an organic order outside the standardized box.

As I was reading an article on an online news site, I chanced upon an advertisement for a beautiful Christmas tree. Indeed, it was an actual Christmas tree, not a holiday, winter, or sparkle tree that celebrates some unknown winter solstice festivity.

This ad unapologetically used the word Christmas, and the tree looked inviting enough to conger up memories of Christmases past. In a nanosecond of Christmas spirit, I clicked on the attractive image and learned about how I might acquire a similar tree for home or office.

The tree, it turns out, is a high-tech, artificial, pre-lit tree that can be sent to your home in a box, wheeled into your living room, and assembled in less than three minutes. Once assembled, using its easy-to-use illustrated instructions, you have nothing left to do but activate the lights with the remote control (batteries included) and stand back to enjoy the stunning beauty of your instant Christmas tree experience.

It would seem there is no easier way to go on the offensive in today's cultural war on Christmas than to fill all places with such trees in any of its six varieties and deck the halls with boughs of synthetic holly!

Far be it for me to criticize any Christmas tree, real or otherwise. In the present cultural climate, any tree that calls itself Christmas is a victory over politically correct conformity. However, I cannot help but think that this pre-lit, ready-to-use, boxed Christmas tree with its "miracle" technology is a fitting symbol of where we have gone wrong in our culture and its celebration of Christ's birth.

We live in a culture of instant gratification where we must have everything right away and effortlessly. This does not only involve indulging in sensual delights, but also our experience of wholesome and uplifting things like Christmas trees.

In our frenzied desire for instant and effortless mass consumption 24/7, we have engaged in what I call the "frenetic intemperance" of throwing off legitimate restraints and engaging in consumption that ignores those cultural and spiritual values that typically serve to temper and give meaning to life.

We have built, it is true, a vast market system that is undoubtedly convenient, plentiful, and inexpensive. In the process, we have sacrificed that human touch that so delights and enriches us. In the name of maximizing efficiency and increasing consumer convenience, a spirit of dreary sameness descends upon the markets. The result is boxes upon boxes of nearly identical high-tech, pre-lit trees that lack soul.

It is this human element that is so essential to the traditional Christmas tree. The spiritual act of creating a unique and marvelous tree still leads millions of Americans to buy real trees and decorate them with a hodge-podge of ornaments and lights. It is precisely the time spent together decorating, and the extra effort involved, that makes the real Christmas tree so unique and memorable... and what makes the three-minute pop-up tree so utterly forgettable.

This human element also confers authenticity and meaning upon the Christmas tree because it becomes an expression of those who prepare it. It gives rise to the creativity of traditional ornaments and wholesome traditions. In other words, the human element brings about true culture and not the pre-packaged substitutes found in so many of today's sterile shopping malls.

Of course, our problem is not just Christmas trees, but a whole culture of unrestraint that has invaded all fields. It leads to rushed schedules and stress-filled lives caused by our impatience with time and space based on the idea that nothing should stand between ourselves and the objects of our gratification. Tethered to our mobile devices, we are constantly feeding a restless desire for new sensations, stimuli, and thrills. When you must have everything instantly and effortlessly, there is the temptation to turn the Christmas season into one more of those sensations. We are encouraged to buy the instant Christmas tree experience rather than experience that special moment called Christmas.

Amid such noisy distractions, there is little time to reflect upon the true peace of Christmas; it is easy to lose track of the "reason for the season": the birth of the Christ Child. In the manger in Bethlehem, we can find the balm that will soothe our agitated souls and take solace, "For a child is born to us, and a son is given to us" (Is. 9:6).

Christmas invites us to reflect upon those things that really matter. In a Christmas-tree-in-a-box culture, it encourages us to think outside the box.

CHAPTER 23

My *Return to Order* Dinner

BY JOHN HORVAT II

Organic solutions unite those who participate in them. When they become part of the culture of a locale, they reflect the ingenuity and resourcefulness of a people. They also become authentic expressions of a unique and special culture. They are so contrary to the standardized products of our days.

As the author of the book, *Return to Order*, I am constantly looking for examples of organic solutions for today's complicated problems. It is one way I can illustrate practically so many of the ideas found in the book. One subject of my search is finding spontaneous expressions of culture that are often destroyed by today's mass standardization. I search out that missing human element in society that makes things warm and inviting.

During a visit to Miami, I chanced upon one such example when invited to a good Spanish-Cuban restaurant in Miami's Little Havana section of town. The place was Spanish enough to represent a taste of all Hispanic countries and Cuban enough to have some connection with the local Cuban community. I unexpectedly found the experience to be one of those *"Return to Order* moments" where you sense something of what a truly organic Christian society was and might still be.

All too often in restaurants, especially chain restaurants, the food does not reflect the people who create it. There are Chinese, Italian, Mexican, or so many other ethnic restaurants that offer their distinctive foods, which are often cooked by and consumed by those outside their communities. While such dining experiences may represent a change of pace to the cosmopolitan diner, there is no real connection between the food and the person. It's just another tasty and satisfying place to eat without context.

However, this Spanish-Cuban restaurant was different. Not only did the food reflect the people who created it, but also those who ate it. Entering the restaurant, I felt immersed into a Hispanic world where people were enjoying and reveling in their own culture. While not Hispanic myself, I sensed a special connection that resonated and united all and communicated a joy which extended even to me.

I was impressed by the authenticity of the place. Much care was taken to create an atmosphere that spoke of tradition and quality. The walls were full of customary plates and jugs. There were pictures and paintings of hunt scenes and country life. The waiters were Spaniards, polite and chivalrous, given to efficient and elegant service. The food was excellent and spicy. The table, with its fine cloth tablecloths and napkins and subdued lighting, invited one to pleasant conversation.

What made this dinner special, though, was the overall tone of the place. There was the exuberant conviviality that comes from being Hispanic that permeated the room. Unlike so many places, where each table is as if in a sealed bubble, people connected with one another. One high point in the meal was when three musicians arrived in Spanish garb. One played guitar, another a high-pitched mandolin, and the third a tambourine. They played and sang Spanish, Cuban, Mexican, and Colombian songs, the audience singing along with peppered cries of "Ole!" As the musicians exited the room, the tambourine man collected donations from satisfied patrons.

In other words, the restaurant satisfied not only our physical appetites, but our spiritual ones as well. It created a warm, human atmosphere full of marvels and beauty that delighted the soul. It presented a unique menu full of flavor and nuance beyond the standardized fare that makes the eating experience bland and boring. It offered not just distinctive dishes, but courtesy, respect, and affection to those who entered. In such an atmosphere, it becomes much easier to engage in delightful conversation with others. The establishment was the expression of a culture and not only that of a bottom line.

While not perfect, the restaurant represented something of that organic Christian society that is essential for a return to order. There was a notion of that close interrelationship that should exist between producers, inhabitants, and the locality to the point that producer and consumer become "co-creators" of goods. There were still remnants of that turning inward by which a people use their local resources to make products suited to their tastes and oriented toward the perfection of their society.

Above all, there was that human element that delights the soul and makes an ordinary meal a *"Return to Order* moment."

CHAPTER 24

In Search of a Calling

BY JOHN HORVAT II

A notion of organic solutions includes the concept of a calling. It would make sense that in a society where everything has purpose and meaning, individuals also discern the God-given meaning of their lives. From childhood forward, people should go about preparing for their futures. In the solitude of reflection, they should follow that calling suited to the passions of their hearts.

At graduation time, college students assemble on campus greens everywhere to mark the occasion. It is a time of hope, joy, and expectation as they enter the next phase of their lives. Beyond a climate of optimism that usually prevails, I cannot help but feel a bit afflicted as these students venture into the real world.

The reason for my affliction is that many of these graduates have yet to find what I would describe as their calling in life. In fact, a sizeable number began their college years without really knowing what they should study, constantly changing majors, and now many leave with a degree unsuited to the desires of their hearts.

It is not by chance that a number of them find unrelated jobs or return unemployed to live with their parents. I often meet or hear of students who have spent fortunes (often that of their parents) and incurred considerable debt at college. Many of these have secured degrees and even advanced degrees in a certain field, yet want to do something else.

One such student graduated in business administration only to find himself selling insurance. What he really wants to be is a writer.

The notion of a calling should be part of everyone's education.

Another person I know is trained to practice in some specialized medical field, yet now works as a gourmet cook (and a very good one at that!). I know several young ladies who have put aside their degrees after only a few years to start a family. Another scrapped his degree and did the unthinkable—he followed in his father's footsteps.

In these cases, there is a mismatch between the degrees these students obtain and the desires of their hearts that they later discover. They go to college because they are told everyone goes to college. As a result, so many of these young people make a $60,000, four-year detour in their lives before figuring out what they desire. More tragic are others that never find what they want and enter into jobs for which they have no passion or liking.

I believe the reason for this mismatch lies in a culture that sets no limits on the individual. The bewildered high school student is told he can be anything, yet is prepared to be nothing. He is overwhelmed by the vast array of choices to the point of indecision.

Adding to the dilemma, college freshmen are told they need not make decisions about their future right away. They can do whatever they please, and, as a result, the university often becomes an extension of childhood where the real decisions of life can be postponed...even until after graduation.

Missing from the lives of these students is the discernment of a calling. Childhood used to be a preparation for adult life. Already from an early age, children were encouraged to ponder the purpose of their lives and prepare themselves for their future by discerning their calling that would correspond to the desires of their hearts.

This calling was easily found in the gentle guidance of parents who noted talents and defects, capabilities and limitations, and pointed their children in the right direction. The discerning child drew upon family traditions, occupations, or reputation. The calling was also heard in the community and parish where representative characters served as models and mentors. The penetrating voice of a parish priest might also present options to the young—including the religious life. In the silence of one's leisure, each could subtly recollect and perceive a unique calling. This discerning process produced inside each soul what Richard Weaver called "the formation of character, the perfection of style, the attainment of distinction in intellect and imagination."

The organic Christian society of times past once nurtured this notion of calling. In such a society, those approaching adulthood already had a general idea of who they were, and what they were to become.

In our times of broken homes and shattered communities, discerning one's calling is challenging, yet not impossible. It takes much more courage and daring to buck the tide and follow the desires of the heart whether it be a degree, a craft or art, or a family.

If I were to have a message, then, for a graduating class, it would be: Leave today's noisy, existential wilderness where you are taught that you have neither place nor purpose in life beyond that of arranging your own pleasure. Leave behind the modern din. Seek your God-given purpose in life. It is not too late to listen for and follow your calling.

Rediscovering the Ideal Healthcare Plan

BY JOHN HORVAT II

Organic solutions work extremely well when combined with Christian charity. People then search for ways to care for and treat their neighbors as themselves for the love of God. This gives rise not only to institutions but whole networks of institutions that solve extremely difficult problems efficiently, economically, and charitably. This was the case of the first real healthcare system, run by religious orders that provided care for the poor and suffering.

There is a prevailing idea that healthcare plans are necessarily complex and expensive schemes. There was, however, an ideal healthcare plan in the distant past that was amazingly simple. The plan did not list its benefits, clinical metrics, or financial data. Its main emphasis was not so much on a *plan* but *care* and the *health* of both body and soul.

Faith Wallis describes this plan in her book called *Medieval Medicine: A Reader*. Looking at this "medieval healthcare plan" is a refreshing glimpse at the kind of care that is sadly lacking today.

By proposing a medieval healthcare plan as an ideal, it does not mean to say that medieval medicine, primitive as it was, is the perfect formula for the present. Medieval medicine was advanced for its time, but certainly not for today. However, the spirit with which people were treated does offer an ideal that can and should be imitated.

Hospitals Return to Roots

Many people do not realize that the hospital as it is known today was an invention of the Middle Ages. They were established from the desire to extend Christian charity to the poor and needy. In the early Middle

Nuns dedicated their lives to God and the cheerful service of all that sought their care.

Ages, hospitals first became attached to monasteries where monks would minister to the sick and dying. No other civilization was able to develop anything remotely comparable.

Medieval hospitals provided free care to the poor and needy. They were usually under the supervision of a religious order that had members with vows of poverty, chastity, and obedience. They dedicated their lives to God and the cheerful service of all that sought their care—including non-Christians.

Not content with those who came to their doors, hospital attendants were regularly obliged to go out into the streets and bring in all those found in need of treatment.

Reception of Patients

The reception of patients was extremely touching in the broad charity extended to them. Every possible effort was made to take care of their spiritual needs. Upon entering the hospital, the patient, when a Catholic, went to confession and received Holy Communion, as the first steps in the healing process. This provided spiritual peace of mind that often had its repercussion in the physical health of the body.

Once admitted, the patient was seen as another Christ. Each was treated as the master of the house, for so each was, according to the hospital's bylaws. Every need was taken care of as if Christ himself were being served.

During a visit to the 2,000-bed Jerusalem Hospital of the Knights of Saint John of Jerusalem, one cleric noted, "It has happened on a number of occasions that when the space...proves insufficient for the multitude of the suffering, the dormitory of the brethren is taken over by the sick and the brethren themselves sleep on the floor."

Those who attended to the care of the sick did not see their role as just a job to be performed. They did not think about their pleasure or profit. They saw their service as something that gave meaning and purpose to their lives. Caring for others was an important means to secure their salvation.

Excellent Care

Thus, the care was as excellent as it could be for the times. Specialists were brought in to take care of extraordinary cases. Doctors made the rounds daily to check on the progress of those in their care. Regulations required that patients should never be left without an attendant and that nurses be on duty at all times, both day and night.

The environment was clean and refreshing. In fact, major works of art were often painted on the hospital walls and ceilings to delight and edify the patients, using the same artistic skills that were employed to adorn churches. Such masterpieces can still be seen today in the buildings that survive.

Particular attention was paid to cleanliness, ventilation, and comfort. Patients were supplied with clean mattresses, white linen sheets, and "fleecy blankets." Care was so excellent that the cleric at the Jerusalem Hospital reported that there were "wealthy people who pretended to be poor to stay in the hospital."

Solicitude for the sick was not limited to the doctors and attendants. Likewise, all Christians saw the sick in a similar Christ-like manner. Patients in ordinary hospitals were often heartened by the visits of persons of high or noble rank and charitable disposition. Visitors might include even personages like Catherine of Sweden; Margaret, Queen of Scotland; or King Saint Louis IX of France.

A Touching Reciprocity

However, the sick were not just the recipients of charity. They also had their duties inside the hospital whereby they extended charity to those around them.

Mindful of how God especially hears the prayers of the suffering, the patients, when Christian, were enjoined to intercede for their benefactors, the authorities, and all in distress. To the extent that they could, theirs was the duty of prayer, Mass attendance, and reception of the Sacraments. At nightfall, the wards might end the day with litanies where the "sick lords" of the house would pray for those in need of prayers. In this way, the sick gave their best to reciprocate for the enormous charity extended to them. Above all, this offering gave meaning and purpose to their suffering.

Hospitals Flourish

As a result of practices like these, the hospitals of the Middle Ages flourished. Every diocese and monastery was encouraged to have hospitals attached to them. The Benedictine order alone is credited with founding 2,000 hospitals. Imbued with this spirit of Christian charity, individuals, guilds, brotherhoods, and municipalities also established and generously endowed hospitals of their own. The result was an extensive system of healthcare that provided for the care of body and soul on a scale never seen before in history.

This impressive system was mostly destroyed by the upheavals of the sixteenth century when the Church and her hospitals were despoiled and plundered. The infamous suppression of the monasteries by England's Henry VIII in 1540 also suppressed the English healthcare system, leaving the poor in misery and putting an end to hospital building in that country for some 200 years.

In modern times, religious orders that once cared for the sick in this manner now face dwindling membership since they adhered to more "up-to-date" theological currents that focus more on quixotic and "liberating" social justice than concrete medical, Christ-like care.

A Lost Ideal Never to Return?

With all the talk about rising premiums and healthcare costs, perhaps it is time to rediscover the ideal medieval healthcare system. The dedicated spirit of this care is so needed in face of today's ever-expanding medical bureaucracies. Perhaps the massive number of complex government regulations and mandates might be better replaced by the selfless work of dedicated men and women who simply treat the sick as if each one is the Person of Christ Himself.

Someone might object that such an ideal system is impossible in today's secular and hedonistic age. People will just not dedicate themselves to the service of the sick and needy. The ideal medieval healthcare plan is a dream that will never again reappear.

This is not true. Religious congregations like the Little Sisters of the Poor are flooded with cheerful young women who minister to the elderly poor in the medieval tradition. Ironically, these same sisters were being prosecuted by the government for failure to comply with government healthcare mandates that would make them complicit in distributing abortion-causing drugs to their employees.

The problem is not the lack of people or even money, but a failure to present the ideal. The ideal healthcare plan will be rediscovered when the Christian Faith is revived in society. Until that return to order comes, there will always be the seeds of this plan inside the Christian souls that await that blessed day.

PART III

The organic solutions we have just described give a very good idea of what can happen when a people develop their personalities and abilities outside frenetic intemperance. Contrary to the mechanistic model introduced by the Industrial Revolution, we can see how the human element, especially when based on the family, can provide a climate that allows a society to flourish.

It gives rise to an incredible variety that is a refreshing contrast to today's standardization. We also saw how these very social relationships inside a community can easily serve as the foundation for an organic economic model that tempers the passions and provides excellent goods and services.

We now turn to the organic economic order itself and seek to furnish examples and models beyond the present rule of money and mere mechanics of commodity exchange. Central to our position is the idea that the foundation of any organic economic model is a passion for justice. This search for justice prevents economics from becoming a means for man to feed his selfish or unbridled passions—or engage in business with frenetic intemperance.

Saint Thomas Aquinas defines the virtue of justice as "to render to each one his own."[1] In economic matters, commutative justice is the particular kind of justice that assures that one party will give to another in transactions what is due in strict equality as, for example, when the price one pays for an apple corresponds to its worth.[2]

An organic Christian economy is based on justice. When justice is the standard, it sets the stage for the other cardinal virtues of prudence, fortitude, and temperance to play their role. It creates the climate for honor and trust to exist between merchant and buyer. Justice naturally tempers markets.

Finally, charity also has a moderating influence on economy in a society in which justice is sought. Naturally, charity cannot govern economic transactions since, for an economy to function justly, each party

---

1. Aquinas, *Summa Theologica*, II-II, q. 58, a. 11.

2. Cf. Ibid., II-II, q. 61.

must be strictly given its due. However, charity does perfect justice because only charity can bring about a true union of hearts and minds.

The examples we present will give readers an idea of how an economy functions without frenetic intemperance. They will show how a climate of justice generates trust and honor. An organic economy is an ideal environment for markets to flourish and for charity to prevail.

CHAPTER 26

The Strong Money of Saint Louis

BY JOHN HORVAT II

A passion for justice should be the true foundation for sound and strong money. The formulae, data, and other economic instruments governing money are necessary, but much more important are the moral principles that are the real backing of money. The lessons of history are especially telling in this regard.

Speaking with a friend recently, we chanced to talk about money and coins. He is a coin collector and had just visited a coin shop nearby. I mentioned my studies of medieval economy and its coinage. Much to my surprise and delight, he reached into his inner coat pocket and pulled out a *gros tournois* coin minted almost 750 years ago in France.

For me, it was something of an emotional experience. I had seen pictures of the coin and knew a bit of its history, but I had never actually held the coin in my hand. When my friend handed it to me, I was thrilled by the chance to "touch history."

The Origin of the Coin

This is no ordinary coin. It is small, slightly larger, yet much thinner than a dime. It is also beautiful with inscriptions and symbols full of meaning upon its faces.

It should be explained that this coin was born of prosperity, since the value of the then-standard denier, or penny, was inconveniently small for use in trade and commerce. Introduced in 1266, this medieval silver coin, worth 12 deniers, provided the added value needed to favor France's expanding economy.

It was called the *gros tournois* because it was minted in the city of Tours—the towers of the city's abbey appear on one of the coin's faces. While many cities in medieval France minted their own *gros* coins, the ones from Tours were among the most stable over the course of centuries.

An Extraordinary Ruler

However, what makes this particular coin very special is the fact that he who minted it was no ordinary person. His name appears in Latin on the coin and reads, "*Ludovicus Rex*," or "Louis the King," also known as Saint Louis.

King Saint Louis IX (1214–1270) was a virtuous ruler beloved by his people and known for his passion for justice and his love of the poor. He became legendary in history for delivering fair judgments to all—rich and poor—who came before him under the tall oak tree of Vincennes.

Good and saintly kings are not only the stuff of legends, but they are also excellent economists. Under his reign, France grew and prospered.

As I held his *gros tournois* in my hand, I could not help but think that we would do well to implement the monetary policies contained in that coin.

A Return to Sound Money

We would do well to go back to sound money. The *gros tournois* was sound money. It was ample in supply, stable in value, beautiful in appearance.

More importantly, the coin did not fulfill the functions of facilitating unbridled credit, frenzied expansion, and speculation, which are so common today. Indeed, such practices were discouraged by the moral codes of the time. The *gros tournois* fulfilled the primary and true functions of money, which should serve as a measure of value, a stable exchange medium, and a temperate store of wealth. In addition, this money did not originate from or thrive upon debt.

The *gros tournois* was a practical and adaptable currency. It was conceived to facilitate the convenience of exchange with common sense, wisdom, and flexibility. It did not dominate over other alternative local currencies. It enjoyed the trust of the people and could be considered a true expression of the culture.

From a purely technical standpoint, the coin represented sound money as defined by many modern economists.

A Return to Moral Money

However, it is not enough to have just sound money if we are to return to order. We would do well to return to moral money.

Saint Louis did not succumb to the temptation of implementing monetary policy based solely on the mechanical manipulations of formulae and numbers. He did not inflate or debase his currency to fit with personal goals.

Modern economists blind themselves to the obvious fact, so often verified, that, in the stormy history of money, bad money most often appears because of the despotic acts of men and rulers. Their good or bad actions determine the course of the economy and the soundness of money.

The *gros tournois* was sound because Saint Louis sought justice. His money enjoyed the trust and confidence of the people because they knew the saintly king would not manipulate or debase it. He used the power and prestige of his office to advance the common good and not his personal affairs.

Money fails when injustice rules and the rule of law is ignored. Then, there is no monetary system that cannot be circumvented or perverted. In vain do we speak about a sound monetary policy outside of virtue. Indeed, virtue is the best backing of money; it far outshines the brilliance of gold.

A Return to Godly Money

Finally, we would do well to return to what might be called "Godly" money, even though such an affirmation might irritate secular people who wish to see God banished from all worldly affairs. The *gros tournois* was Godly money. Upon one of its faces, there is a large cross of Christ. The abbreviated inscription on the front says in Latin, "*Benedictum sit nomen domini nostri Jesu Christi*," or, "Blessed be the name of Our Lord Jesus Christ."

It is proper that even money should call to mind God and our last ends. Meditating on our salvation puts our desires and appetites in order, which in turn tempers the frenzied excesses of unrestraint in an economy. The cross on the coin signifies the fact that money cannot take away the suffering and trials of our fallen nature. It cannot buy happiness.

During that age of Faith, it was not unreasonable to think that when the name of Jesus Christ is blessed upon coinage, Christ's blessings upon the economy can be expected, as indeed happened in Saint Louis's times.

Confiding in Government

Alas, in our age of disbelief, people today prefer to put their faith in the Federal Reserve and central banks—from which no blessings flow. Rather than throw themselves upon their knees, people prefer to throw themselves into the frenetic intemperance of modern markets that encourages instant gratification and unbridled indulgence.

When frenzied economies fail, as they inevitably do, they call upon massive governments to prop them up, accumulate debt, and destroy yet further the currencies of the land.

Would that we might return to the wise policies of Saint Louis! History records that when money suffered debasement from wars and unsound policies in fourteenth century France, the people clamored and longed for the "strong money" of good King Saint Louis.

Holding the *gros tournois* in my hand, I, too, found myself clamoring for the strong money of Good King Saint Louis. It is still strong.

CHAPTER 27

Natural Law Exists. . .Even for Hackers

BY JOHN HORVAT II

Any discussion of justice must include the necessity of law. Without law, economy and society would not be able to function. This is especially true of natural law. Security systems and firewalls are all very important to the functioning of our technological world. However, it is the notion of natural law and its insistence that objective standards of right and wrong exist that prevent the collapse of society. A passion for justice is a foundation for a safe society and a vibrant economy, as this example will show.

Internet security has left me with many concerns, especially as I meet more and more people who have had their accounts hacked or vital information stolen. Despite all the security measures companies may take to keep bad people honest, the sad fact is there are plenty of people out there who break into these systems and make our lives miserable.

When we hack down the moral firewalls that restrain us, we also take down the supporting pillars that prevent society's collapse.

The typical response of the industry is to heap on even more complex security and firewalls. However, I believe that the best firewalls are the moral firewalls inside souls that recognize the distinctions between good and evil and lead us to act accordingly. When those moral walls go down, there are no possible means to keep everything secure.

My security concerns were only confirmed during a recent plane trip. As I made my way down the aisle to my seat in the aircraft, I saw a young, bearded, twenty-something man next to my seat. I noticed his bubbly temperament, which almost guaranteed an in-flight conversation. I also noted that he was incredibly adept at manipulating his iPhone.

True to my expectation, we soon engaged in a conversation after takeoff. I introduced myself as a writer, and he promptly identified himself as a hacker.

A hacker? Yes, but, of course, he was a "good" hacker that works on the other side of the hacking equation. He is paid by companies to hack into their systems to verify their security measures.

The hacker was an amiable fellow, but he was all nervousness as he constantly fidgeted with his devices. He spoke incredibly fast, as it seemed his mind was working much more quickly than his ability to speak. It was as if he were all impulse. Over the course of our conversation, he explained his hacker's creed to me—a philosophy of life apparently shared by many fellow hackers on both sides of the equation.

Hackers, he explained, question everything, doubt everything, and are irreverent to all that is sacred. They trust no one and decide everything by their own standards. They live life intensely, as if that is all there is, and hence do not acknowledge any religious considerations. They accept only those limits needed to survive in a frenzied world and are always pushing the envelope.

Such a creed only facilitates the task of hacking, since it creates in the person an obsessive desire to break down barriers and challenge all structures. When I asked the hacker what kind of systems he hacked, he replied, not without a little pride, that he had entered all sorts of systems almost with impunity. He entered one banking system and removed $100,000 and reconciled the ledger without the bank noticing. He even hacked a railroad transport system and commandeered a freight train from his laptop. Hackers, he claimed, could bring the whole system down if they so wished.

I then asked him why, if it could be done, the hackers did not take down the system. He replied that hackers fear severe legal penalties, especially in the post-9/11 world. He also claimed the best hackers (like him) are very well paid by the business establishment.

However, I found these answers a bit unconvincing since they do not include terrorists, anarchists, and enemies who are constantly probing our systems and making our world a dangerous place.

The better answer came when I asked why he, in particular, did not bring the whole system down, since the hackers' creed pretty much allows and even encourages such behavior. It was then that a moral firewall kicked in. Although he found it hard to define right and wrong, he said he felt it would be wrong to do something of this nature.

Such moral firewalls, weak though they may be in the souls of post-modern men, are still our best and only defense against chaos. Just as no police force in the world can stop a whole population intent upon stealing, so also no security system can thwart a network of unscrupulous hackers determined to create cyber chaos. Moral restraint on the part of most people keeps society in order. Remnants of such restraint hold back even the hackers from bringing on Armageddon.

I was struck how the hackers' creed was consistent with the frenetic intemperance of our culture which likewise accepts no restraint and breaks down barriers. Not only are our computer systems at risk, but all modern-day systems—whether financial, infrastructural, or educational—are vulnerable when moral restraint is gone. The more complex and interconnected our systems become, the greater the risks when they fail.

When we hack down the moral firewalls that restrain us, we also take down the supporting pillars that prevent society's collapse. That is why a return to order is only possible when the moral issues are restored. If everyone adopts the hackers' creed, society will be like a commandeered train heading toward the cliff.

CHAPTER 28

What Does Saint Thomas Say about Immigration?

BY JOHN HORVAT II

Society should have a passion for justice that applies to all fields of social and economic life. In medieval Christendom, there was a zealous concern that all received their due. When this was done, organic solutions appeared that were full of common sense and justice. When people have a passion for justice, there are solutions for everything—even sticky modern problems like immigration.

In looking at the debate over immigration, it is almost automatically assumed that the Church's position is one of unconditional charity toward those who enter the nation, legally or illegally.

However, is this the case? What does the Bible say about immigration? What do Church doctors and theologians say? Above all, what does the greatest of doctors, Saint Thomas Aquinas, say about immigration? Does his opinion offer some insights into the burning issues now shaking the nation and blurring our borders?

Immigration is a modern problem, and so some might think that the medieval Saint Thomas would

Saint Thomas Aquinas

have no opinion about the problem, and yet he does. One has only to look in his masterpiece, the *Summa Theologica*, in the first part of the second part, question 105, article 3. There one finds his analysis based on biblical insights that can add to the national debate. They are entirely applicable to the present. Such insights will be submitted here and followed by a brief commentary.

Saint Thomas: "Man's relations with foreigners are twofold: peaceful, and hostile: and in directing both kinds of relation the Law contained suitable precepts."

Commentary: In making this affirmation, Saint Thomas affirms that not all immigrants are equal. Every nation has the right to decide which immigrants are beneficial, that is, "peaceful," to the common good. As a matter of self-defense, the State can reject those criminal elements, traitors, enemies, and others who it deems harmful or "hostile" to its citizens.

The second thing he affirms is that the manner of dealing with immigration is determined by law in the cases of both beneficial and "hostile" immigration. The State has the right and duty to apply its law.

Saint Thomas: "For the Jews were offered three opportunities of peaceful relations with foreigners. First, when foreigners passed through their land as travelers. Secondly, when they came to dwell in their land as newcomers. And in both these respects the Law made kind provision in its precepts: for it is written (Exodus 22:21): 'Thou shalt not molest a stranger [*advenam*—stranger as passing through]'; and again (Exodus 22:9): 'Thou shalt not molest a stranger [*peregrine*—stranger as pilgrim].'"

Commentary: Here Saint Thomas acknowledges the fact that others will want to come to visit or even stay in the land for some time. Such foreigners deserved to be treated with charity, respect, and courtesy, which is due to any human of good will. In these cases, the law can and should protect foreigners from being mistreated or molested.

Saint Thomas: "Thirdly, when any foreigners wished to be admitted entirely to their fellowship and mode of worship. With regard to these, a certain order was observed. For they were not at once admitted to citizenship: just as it was law with some nations that no one was deemed a citizen except after two or three generations, as the Philosopher says (Polit. iii, 1)."

Commentary: Saint Thomas recognizes that there will be those who will want to stay and become citizens of the lands they visit. However, he sets as the first condition for acceptance a desire to integrate fully into what would today be considered the culture and life of the nation.

A second condition is that the granting of citizenship would not be immediate. The integration process takes time. People need to adapt themselves to the nation. He quotes the philosopher Aristotle as saying this process was once deemed to take two or three generations. Saint Thomas himself does not give a timeframe for this integration, but he does admit that it can take a long time.

Saint Thomas: "The reason for this was that if foreigners were allowed to meddle with the affairs of a nation as soon as they settled down in its midst, many dangers might occur since the foreigners not yet having the common good firmly at heart might attempt something hurtful to the people."

Commentary: The common sense of Saint Thomas is certainly not politically correct, but it is logical. The theologian notes that living in a nation is a complex thing. It takes time to know the issues affecting the nation. Those familiar with the long history of their nation are in the best position to make the long-term decisions about its future. It is harmful and unjust to put the future of a place in the hands of those recently arrived, who, although through no fault of their own, have little idea of what is happening or has happened in the nation. Such a policy could lead to the destruction of the nation.

As an illustration of this point, Saint Thomas later notes that the Jewish people did not treat all nations equally since those nations closer to them were more quickly integrated into the population than those who were not as close. Some hostile peoples were not to be admitted at all into full fellowship due to their enmity toward the Jewish people.

Saint Thomas: "Nevertheless it was possible by dispensation for a man to be admitted to citizenship on account of some act of virtue: thus it is related (Judith 14:6) that Achior, the captain of the children of Ammon, 'was joined to the people of Israel, with all the succession of his kindred.'"

Commentary: That is to say, the rules were not rigid. Some exceptions were granted based on the circumstances. However, such exceptions were not arbitrary but always had in mind the common good. The example of Achior describes the citizenship bestowed upon the captain and his children for the good services rendered to the nation.

* * *

These are some of the thoughts of Saint Thomas Aquinas on the matter of immigration based on biblical principles. It is clear that immigration must have two things in mind: the first is the nation's unity, and the second is the common good.

Immigration should have as its goal integration, not disintegration or segregation. The immigrant should not only desire to assume the benefits but the responsibilities of joining into the full fellowship of the nation. By becoming a citizen, a person becomes part of a broad family over the long term and not a shareholder in a joint-stock company seeking only short-term self-interest.

Secondly, Saint Thomas teaches that immigration must have in mind the common good; it cannot destroy or overwhelm a nation.

This explains why so many Americans experience uneasiness caused by massive and disproportional immigration. Such policy artificially introduces a situation that destroys common points of unity and overwhelms the ability of a society to absorb new elements organically into a unified culture. The common good is no longer considered.

A proportional immigration has always been a healthy development in a society since it injects new life and qualities into a social body, but when it loses that proportion and undermines the purpose of the State, it threatens the well-being of the nation.

When this happens, the nation would do well to follow the advice of Saint Thomas Aquinas and biblical principles. The nation must practice justice and charity towards all, including foreigners, but it must above all safeguard the common good and its unity, without which no country can long endure.

CHAPTER 29

Jewelry Shop Economics

BY JOHN HORVAT II

A passion for justice generates a passion for excellence in economy. This enables people to see beyond profit and build relationships of trust. In such an economy, people make or sell quality goods. They stand behind them and provide service, often without charge. When this valuable human element enters into economy, everyone benefits.

Quite by accident, I came to frequent a jewelry store that would help me take care of those small problems with watches that can be so vexing. I was tired of department store attendants who could not replace batteries or change watch bands. It seemed that every time I took a watch in to be fixed, it was cheaper to get it replaced.

That is when I decided to visit a jewelry shop. It was the "little things" that impressed me. I was struck by how they took such care in doing things right. They served the customer with great skill and solicitude. Even their little paper bags with roped handles had a special charm. When I showed them my old department store watch, they proposed a reasonably priced, American-assembled watch with their name on it. I knew I could trust them to back up their name. I was even told that they would replace the battery free of charge for as long as I owned the watch.

Over the years, this watch has served me well. My jewelers have never let me down. After all, it is "their" watch; it has their name on it. Whenever there is a problem, I bring it to the shop, and they take care of it, usually without charge. On my part, I spread the word that there is a good jewelry shop in town that treats people well.

Recently, the watch's battery went dead, and I rushed over to get it fixed before traveling out of state. I entered the small shop and was greeted from behind the counter. An atmosphere of pride and professionalism permeates the store. I am impressed by the dazzling displays of beautiful and marvelous jewels. Through a window, one can see the workshop where the master jeweler works with his highly magnified and thick glasses so as to better see the jewels he fixes.

I presented my powerless watch to the lady at the counter who took it to a room in the back to do the relatively simple job of replacing the battery.

It was then that the "little things" started to happen—those things that keep me coming back. After a short time, she returned to say that the battery was replaced but that the small rubber gasket on the back was starting to come apart and that it should be replaced. She enlisted the help of John, the master jeweler, who took it to his workshop and replaced the gasket free of charge. When he returned the watch, he asked me if I wore the watch on the right or left wrist. I replied that it was the left wrist. He then said that if that was the case, the buckle on the leather watchband should be on the other side and promptly changed it. We exchanged pleasantries, and I left the store.

During my encounter at the jewelry shop, not much commercial exchange took place. We did not stimulate the economy. In fact, they received no money from me. However, I did give them my trust, and they reciprocated by giving me excellent service. We strengthened a precious relationship that money cannot buy.

My experience with the watch was for me a very practical lesson in the way economy should be. It should be built upon justice, honor, and trust. There needs to be that human element by which people show genuine concern and a desire to serve others. There needs to be that passion for doing things well and right. Such things may not appear quantified in the bottom line, but they are the foundation for good business.

I cannot help but think that this is what is missing in today's frenzied markets. Everything is so focused on the big things: sales, massive production, and quarterly earnings reports. The human element gets left out. If we are to return to a balanced economic order, more "little things" need to happen.

CHAPTER 30

Cobbler Shop Economics

BY JOHN HORVAT II

A passion for justice generates a sense of craftsmanship, quality, and pride in one's work. In an economy based on justice, people stand behind their work and live off their good reputations. Frenetic intemperance becomes difficult in such markets and everything enters into balance.

I had just bought a pair of shoes at a large shoe outlet, and within six months the heels were completely worn down. I lost the receipt and probably would have had a little trouble getting a new pair, so I decided to visit the local cobbler with the shoes and a piece of leather carry-on luggage with a broken latch. I only expected him to fix my things, but came out with a lesson in economy.

The cobbler shop is just off the main street in a small Pennsylvania town nearby. It is an unassuming building where you can walk in from the sidewalk and the bells on the doors announce your arrival. The cobbler lives in semi-retirement nearby. He is open on afternoons to any who need his services and to all his friends who just want to come around and talk.

Upon entering, the first thing you see is a counter with an old-fashioned cash register and all sorts of leather products with an order known only to the cobbler himself. There is something warm and familiar about the whole scene, which is permeated by the smell of leather. On one side there are some shelves where you can buy a strange array of unclaimed items. Visible in the back is the workshop with its stitching machines where the actual cobbling is done.

The cobbler is an older gentleman with a round face who greets me with ease. We exchange some small talk and then enter into the business at hand. I present my shoes, and he looks at them and delivers his diagnosis.

"Worn heels, I guess I could put a pair on for you," he says. He takes out a small square of paper and writes my phone number on it, makes a hole in the paper and threads one of the shoe laces through it. He gives me no receipt to show that he has my shoes. I must trust him, and I do.

© Wavebreakmedia Ltd | Dreamstime.com

You could feel the sense of craftsmanship, quality and pride in his work.

He looks at my carry-on with the broken latch. That proves a bit more difficult. He opens up a little cabinet and pulls out some latches. None of them will work, and so he ponders the situation for a while, looking at it this way and that.

"Snaps," he says pensively, "I could put on some snaps." He shows me how he would attach them to the bag to make it easy to open. We discuss the matter and come to an agreement. I must return sometime next week.

Leaving the cobbler shop, I thought a bit about what had just happened, not from the point of view of footwear, but from the perspective of the economic studies I have long pursued. Here was an example of economy without that frenetic intemperance that you find in so many parts of modern markets. There was nothing of that frenzied sense of immediacy where you must have everything right away, regardless of the consequence. I did not sense that machine-like treatment that makes so much of modern economy cold and impersonal, fast and frantic.

Instead, my visit had that human element that made the experience warm and personal. I was a valued customer, not a number. He became *my* cobbler. I appreciated the trust that was the basis of our transaction, and which is so essential for any free market. Above all, there was a notion of honor. You could feel the sense of craftsmanship, quality, and pride in his work. He would stand behind his work as he has for decades. He does not need to advertise since he lives off his good reputation.

Some might object that the cobbler is a figure from the past that has no role in modern economy. Today's markets with their cheap goods have eliminated the need for such professions. When something breaks, just buy another one. There is no demand for cobblers anymore.

Yet, I would disagree. At least in my area, people are looking for them. The old cobblers are dying off in the region and the unemployed new generations (anxious perhaps for more exciting careers) no longer want to commit to such a profession. I was told that my cobbler laments the fact that he can find no one to take his place in the face of obvious demand.

I am not suggesting that everyone should run their business like my cobbler. However, I am suggesting that we should return to an order where trust, honor, and temperance can prevail again.

In this sense, I cannot help but think of the economic good my cobbler has done by plying his trade. Without the cobbler, I would have been forced to buy another cheap, seventy-dollar pair of shoes made in India and an expensive carry-on leather portfolio from who knows where.

As it turned out, while putting the snaps on the portfolio, the old broken latch fell out of one of the compartments. He just fixed it and charged nothing for the effort. Thus, I spent some fifteen dollars for the repairs...and the human experience. The whole affair had a calming effect on me and the economy since it tempers that frenetic desire of buying without restraint or reflection that sooner or later leads to frenzied and failed markets.

That is what I learned from a visit to my cobbler and my accidental lesson in economy. If there were more cobblers and fewer derivative traders, I believe the world would be a calmer and richer place.

CHAPTER 31

The Bank that Trust Built

BY JOHN HORVAT II

When there is a passion for justice, it facilitates the building of trust in economy and society. This can happen in any sector of the economy—even in banking. This is a case from England that demonstrates that not only is it possible to bank without frenetic intemperance, but that it can be done profitably over generations. This becomes possible when there are strong moral values and a desire to serve.

In writing about economy, I have frequently denounced a restless and reckless spirit inside some areas of modern economy that I call frenetic intemperance. This is often found in the financial sector, as it engages in all sorts of monetary wheeling and dealing.

I admit that banks have their purpose in society by securing money and facilitating transactions needed to carry out business. However, so strong is the frantic idea of modern banking that I have often asked myself if I could provide concrete examples of banking without frenetic intemperance. It is not an easy task.

Upon traveling to Ireland, though, I came upon the business section of *The Sunday Times* (7/21/2013). I quite unexpectedly found a refreshing example that revealed a passion for justice and excellence. It involves a London bank called C. Hoare & Co. It is not your ordinary bank.

This is a 345-year-old institution run by a family. The bank's senior partner is Henry Hoare, one of seven family partners who are all 10th—or 11th—generation descendants of bank founder Richard Hoare.

"Our aim is to treat others as we would wish to be treated."
—*Sir Richard Hoare*

"Founded in 1672, we remain wholly owned by the Hoare family and continue to be guided and led by the descendants of the bank's founder," reads the bank's website. "We have no allegiance to any other institution. Our aim is to treat others as we would wish to be treated."

Just this statement alone would be enough to set the bank apart from all others, but there is more. This bank assumes unlimited liability for its actions. If a mistake is made, the bank pays the cost.

Needless to say, with such a conservative policy in force, not many mistakes are made. Perhaps that helps explain why the bank has an extensive list of distinguished past clients that includes Samuel Pepys, Lord Byron, and Jane Austen.

Someone might object that such a bank is only a picturesque relic of past times and time-honored tradition. What about the bottom line? Does this bank make money?

It appears its conservative policies in such frenetic and uncertain times pay off. Business is booming. Since the financial crisis of 2008 began, the deposit base of the bank has doubled to £2.3 billion ($3.55 billion). Deposits are increasing monthly.

Modern marketers might imagine that the bank must use its traditional image to attract these new customers and aid expansion. This is hardly the case. In fact, it seems that the bank does everything possible not to grow and expand.

The bank has always maintained only two branches over the centuries and has no interest in going beyond this number. It has never used a marketing plan to attract customers. The bank offers interest rates to savers that are paltry. There is even a service charge of £60 ($93) a month for those with an average monthly balance of less than £25,000 ($38,600), yet new customers are banging at the door in droves to open accounts.

The key to success is the very active role of the family in all aspects of the bank's operation, especially the lending part. Because they must assume full liability for their transactions, the Hoare family is very careful in selecting its family partners. Some 1,000 Hoare descendants could qualify to be partners, but there is a strict vetting process that makes sure only the most capable ascend to the top. The family puts aside funds to invest for future generations. It also donates generously to the family charity.

This stable yet profitable bank engages in wise investment policy quite different from those policies found all over the world of finance. Only half of the bank's deposits are loaned out while another quarter is safely lodged at the Bank of England. Customers know they can trust the firm not to engage in transactions that have unnecessary exposure to risk.

Thus, banking, like any other business, can exist without frenetic intemperance. Such banks can even flourish and be very profitable. This London bank shows how the family can be an important instrument to temper business and keep it in balance. Hoare & Co. proves it does not have to be a dog-eat-dog world. All it takes is a little temperance.

PART IV REPRESENTATIVE CHARACTERS

We have presented examples of organic solutions and the passion for justice as part of our proposal for an organic Christian society. However, the key to any society lies in its members. There must be those extraordinary people who rise above their own self-interest and help others to live together in virtue and serve God.

Sociologists call these people representative characters. They are those who perceive the ideals, principles, and qualities that are desired and admired by a family, community, or nation, and translate them into concrete programs of life and culture.

Representative figures are all around us. We might point to famous figures like General George Patton or those lesser known people such as self-sacrificing clergy, devoted teachers, or selfless community leaders who draw and fuse society together and set the tone for their respective social groups. Organic Christian society needs legions of these representative characters if it is to prosper. The idea of a single leader who will solve everything is not enough.

Modern culture discourages the idea of representative characters and proposes false and unrepresentative characters that glorify self-gratification and help promote a mass society. Because these unrepresentative characters appear to dominate the culture, many have the impression that true representative characters are rare and hard to find.

However, these characters do exist everywhere if we know where to look. They are found in humble places or positions of leadership. They are especially found in families in which fathers and mothers sacrifice themselves for the sake of their children. These principled people are often found where one least expects.

Heroes are another category of people that can be representatives. For this reason, many representative figures are found in the armed forces. The battlefield brings out the best in men.

The following selection is far from comprehensive, but it will give an idea of what kind of person is needed. There will be no return to order unless people from all walks of life step up to the plate and do their duty. The stories told here serve as an invitation to all readers to be part of the solution by either being a representative character or supporting such figures wherever they might appear.

CHAPTER 32

Shirley at the Plate

BY JOHN HORVAT II

Representative characters are not only found in high places. They exist at all levels of society, even the humblest. What is remarkable about these figures is that they can interpret and put into action the aspirations of those around them. In this way, they form the most dynamic part of a culture and help a people express themselves.

As we entered the parking shuttle at Los Angeles International Airport, my two colleagues and I politely greeted the driver, a cheerful, grandmotherly black lady. We were the only ones on the shuttle, and, as we sat down, it seemed like a good opportunity to engage in a bit of light conversation.

Her name was Shirley, and she had that kind of exuberant, joyful disposition toward life that was contagious. We asked her about her job, and she said she was happy about it for three reasons: she likes people; she likes to drive; and she likes to work outdoors. This job was perfect, so she had no complaints, no resentments, and plenty of common sense.

However, while Shirley was content with her job, she was not completely oblivious to what was happening in the nation. She was not a self-centered person only concerned about her little world. She knew a lot about the problems inside society, and she was quite outspoken about them.

When she asked what we were doing, we explained our activism in defense of moral values and God. The mention of God hit a sensitive point, and she came alive. She decried the loss of faith and the moral crisis of our days, and talked at length about them. She was very opinionated, and many of those opinions were not politically correct.

She was indignant, for example, that "In God We Trust" was taken off the face of the Susan B. Anthony one-dollar coin—it was put on the rim of the coin instead. "I tell people, 'If you get one of 'em, give it back and ask for a dollar bill,'" she commented.

"People need to step up to the plate," Shirley told us. "It only took one woman to take prayer out of the schools. Everyone thought it would be impossible, but that one woman got it through because no one opposed her. We need to speak out."

As we approached our terminal, Shirley apologized, saying it was time for her to "get off my soap box." However, on our part, there was no need to apologize since we were all edified by her attitude. It was evident to me that she was a person who influenced those around her.

Shirley is someone that sociologists call "representative characters." They are natural leaders who embody the values of those around them and put them into a plan of action. They are people who step up to the plate.

Usually, when referring to these characters, we tend to think of people with a lot of money, position, or prestige. That is not always the case. On the parking shuttle, we found a refreshing example of a representative character from much humbler origins. I have no doubt that she plays a role that is not small where she lives and works.

Indeed, that our nation is not in worse shape is only because there are all sorts of natural leaders like Shirley all over the country who climb onto their soap boxes. However, these existing figures are not enough to change the course of the nation. What we will need if we are to return to order are legions of heroes to come forth and let their voices be heard. We will need many more Shirleys to step up to the plate.

CHAPTER 33

The Father Figure as He Should Be

BY JOHN HORVAT II

The family is a natural setting for representative characters. Both the father and mother figures have an important role in molding a family identity. The father figure provides direction and protection. It is only natural that society will need many good fathers if there is to be a return to order. Indeed, society will need true patriarchs, the father figure as he should be.

The figure of the father is under attack these days. To those who insist upon total equality, he is seen as an overbearing figure who has long abused his power. Like all symbols of authority, he must be overthrown.

It is curious that whenever feminists wish to attack the father, somewhere in their long tirades there will appear the word "patriarchy." The mention of this word is not by chance. It echoes the core of the feminist creed.

Ironically, those who are accused of defending patriarchy are usually members of nuclear families, not patriarchal ones. Many indeed are not even members of extended families. They do not have a notion of what patriarchy means and how it functions, and thus they are not in conditions to defend themselves against the feminist rage.

Saint Louis Martin, father of Saint Thérèse of the Child Jesus, brought up his daughters in the holy fear of God.

Embracing Patriarchy

Those who defend the family have no cause to fear the term and every reason to embrace it. When stripped of its non-Christian forms and feminist caricatures, patriarchy becomes a refreshing idea. Even today, the image of an ancient patriarch evokes sentiments of veneration and respect. However, there is a reason why feminists attack patriarchy so violently: It represents the plenitude of fatherhood. It is the father figure as he should be. Such a vision is part of the natural hierarchical society that feminism rejects.

Understanding Patriarchy

The key to understanding patriarchy lies in the long forgotten idea of the traditional family. The Catholic Church has long taught that the family is not a single social unit existing in the present without connection to the past or future. Rather, the family is a rich and continuous whole that encompasses all those who have come before and will come after. Thus, each family becomes a vast network of interwoven relationships and is part of the social fabric.

Patriarchy is a natural consequence of the traditional family. It holds that since this vast social unit exists, there should be an authority that maintains its unity. This authority is usually the patriarch.

The influence of the patriarch extends beyond his immediate household and encompasses several generations. It might include several branches of the family, even an entire clan.

The patriarch does not exercise an arbitrary or tyrannical authority. Indeed, he exerts a unifying leadership over the whole that is expressed more often by influence than by command. He guides with great care and subtlety the interrelationships between so many people who are alike in so many ways, but who are also so very different.

The Patriarch as Harmonizer

Thus one of the most important roles of the patriarch is to be a harmonizer. He maintains the family line in harmony with its past and future. He must strike a delicate balance between those in the family who guarantee necessary continuity and those who energetically introduce healthy innovation.

The patriarch is a true leader of the family. He has a special gift to discern and coordinate the general direction of those under him. He seldom imposes his will upon the others, but rather sets the tone and the example. He unifies and brings out the best in others.

That is why traditionally the patriarch is portrayed as one who ponders things. He is judicious and weighs matters with criteria and acumen. He applies the family's treasure-trove of wisdom which is preserved, enriched, and passed on from one generation to the next.

Source of Progress and Culture

It is easy to see that when society is filled with patriarchal figures on all social levels, it creates the ideal conditions for the true progress of a culture. The patriarch is a representative character who moves his family members toward goals of perfection in line with the family's qualities and talents. When imbued with Catholic virtue, the patriarch moves his family members to the highest of all goals: their sanctification.

Such figures are sadly missing in today's crumbling society. Individuals each go their way. There are no harmonizers or coordinators that unify families and direct their progress.

When attacked for being patriarchal, fathers today should embrace the idea. The patriarch only does on a larger scale that which the father is called to do within his family.

There is nothing wrong with building a family from a long-term perspective. There is nothing wrong with desiring unity and direction for those under one's care. Rather than an undesirable condition to be avoided, patriarchy is an idea whose restoration time has come.

CHAPTER 34

Tillman's Tower

BY NORMAN FULKERSON

Representative characters are those who go beyond the call of duty. They represent virtues and hopes desired by a people. Thus, we need heroes to express who we are as a people. Americans are very attracted to military role models. In our materialistic age, we are touched by the selflessness of those who gave all. Generous figures like these move people to sacrifice and noble actions. They represent an essential part of any return to order.

I n the center of West Point's historic campus in upstate New York stands a statue of Gen. Douglas MacArthur. Below him is a plaque bearing the words of wisdom he once spoke: "On the fields of friendly strife are sown the seeds that upon other fields, on other days, shall bear the fruits of victory."

No one understood these words better than Pat Tillman, a former professional football player. He died April 22, 2004, on another field, when his 2nd Battalion, 75th Regiment unit was ambushed in its efforts to chase down Osama Bin Laden during Operation Mountain Storm in southeast Afghanistan.

General Douglas MacArthur Statue, United States Military Academy, West Point,

Of all the details I read about this extraordinary man's life, one anecdote seemed to stand out and define him. Mark Brand, a friend of Tillman and Assistant Athletic Director at Arizona State University, related how Tillman would often sneak into the University's football stadium after hours and climb to the top of a 200-foot light tower. "He would sit in the basket and study, ponder, and think," he said. "I can't tell you how dangerous that was."

The fact that it was risky obviously did not matter to Pat Tillman. In his search for a higher ideal, he wanted to escape everything, even the football field, dwarfed below him. Pat Tillman was a very good football player. However, he was studying something much higher than play-books in his tower atop Sun Devil Stadium. He was studying life.

He received a marketing degree in three-and-a-half years that some said would take five. He graduated *summa cum laude* with an impressive 3.84 grade point average. According to fellow student, Ed Odeven, "When he wasn't studying the finer points of, say, advertising campaigns, he was reading lengthy philosophy books, sometimes a few at a time."[1]

With so many athletes appearing in courtrooms these days, it is un-believably refreshing to see someone of Tillman's caliber uphold higher principles. It is so rare to see higher values like honor, loyalty, and un-selfishness in mortals of the twenty-first century.

What Motivated This Man?

It was not football or money. He gave them both up to join the army, taking a pay cut of close to $3.5 million to do so. It was not cheering fans. Tim Layden, a senior writer for *Sports Illustrated*, wrote, "Pat was the kind of guy who would rather play football in a parking lot than in a stadium with 100,000 people watching."[2]

No, Pat Tillman was a man in search of a dream. He wanted some-thing higher than himself and would not allow anything to get in his way. Arizona State University Coach Bruce Snyder found this out the hard way when he suggested red-shirting Tillman because he was not big enough, tall enough, or fast enough to make the team as a freshman.

According to Mark Brand, Pat looked the veteran coach in the eye: "You can red-shirt me, or you can play me. It's your choice; but I am not going to be around after four years. I have a life to live."

Something Not Seen since the Forties

For too long now, people have had to put up with whimpering "under-paid" athletes. Many are starting to realize that, in a war-torn world where terrorism is the constant threat, there might be something of greater value than million-dollar salaries.

Pat Tillman comes along and does something unheard of since the forties, when, during the war, athletes and actors alike joined the mil-itary in large numbers. Baseball great Ted Williams simply requested a

---

1. Ed Odeven, "Tillman Touched Many," *Arizona Daily Sun,* Apr. 24, 2004.

2. "Ex-NFL Star Pat Tillman Dies in Afghanistan," Fox News, Apr. 23, 2004.

deferment, and public opinion castigated him for it. That is because the public expected men to enlist at that time, but not today.

When visiting the ASU web page, I saw a picture of a little boy standing in front of a memorial dedicated to Tillman. He was all alone, gazing up in admiration at his hero. In a world where roles models are few and far between, Tillman stands alone. He is someone a father could point out to his son and say, "That is Pat Tillman, the NFL great who turned his back on fame and fortune to serve his country in time of need."

Turns Down Millions out of Loyalty

He could then tell all the facts that leave one almost speechless. He was drafted by the Arizona Cardinals in the seventh round, almost at rock bottom, but through sheer determination made a name for himself. Subsequently, he was offered a $9 million contract with the newly crowned Super Bowl champions, the St. Louis Rams. Tillman's agent Frank Bauer was stunned when he turned it down. "He said he wanted to remain loyal to the people who were loyal to him," Bauer said.[3]

The day after the September 11 attacks, that loyalty manifested itself again. While the nation wept over the dead, Tillman reflected on family members who had served their country, and expressed his need to follow their example. "My great-grandfather was at Pearl Harbor, and a lot of my family has...gone and fought in wars, and I really haven't done a thing as far as laying myself on the line like that."[4]

He went on to make his family and country proud by following his words with action. He did not just don a uniform and carry a gun, however; he went all out by joining the elite Rangers where a good percentage of those who try out fail. This did not surprise those who knew him. Before the 2000 NFL season, Tillman ran a marathon "just to see what it would be like." Evidently, he liked it. The next year he ran a 70-mile triathlon as a warm-up for the 2001 season.

A Sacrifice Worthy of Recognition

Although most Americans are edified by the selflessness of Pat Tillman, others are strangely uncomfortable having the spotlight on one

---

3. Paola Boivin, "Pat Tillman: One Man, one sacrifice," *The Arizona Republic*, Apr. 24, 2004.

4. "Ex-NFL star Tillman Makes 'Ultimate Sacrifice,'" NBC, MSNBC news services, Apr. 26, 2004, accessed Jun. 7, 2017, http://msnbc.msn.com/id/4815441.

individual. The great sin of today is not being different (we have plenty of those). It is to be more.

Tillman admirably made the decision to join the army and did so discreetly, refusing interviews and media coverage out of a desire to be anonymous like everyone else.

"He viewed his decision," said Arizona Sen. John McCain, "as no more patriotic than that of his less fortunate, less renowned countrymen."

The *New York Times* writer Harvey Araton counsels his readers to "respect" Tillman's wishes for anonymity since "nothing could more trivialize the mounting deaths of those less fortunate and less renowned... than the tossing around of clichés like footballs on the virtues of one man's heroism and sacrifice."[5]

Such a commentary misses the point entirely. In the name of justice, tribute must be paid to honor the life and the death of someone that was not like all the rest, and therefore deserved to be singled out and recognized.

Thank God for Pat Tillman

I do not deny that there was a spicier side of this former athlete. This should not be imitated. However, focusing on the unselfish sacrifice he made for his country, many young people today and in the future who thirst for role models have found one in Pat Tillman.

Cpl. Pat Tillman, former NFL football player, died in combat in Afghanistan fighting for his country.

Gen. George S. Patton—another hero not known for his blandness—once said that it was wrong to mourn the death of men like Tillman. "Rather we should thank God that such men lived."

Were I as courageous as he, I would climb to the top of "Tillman's Tower" high above Sun Devil Stadium and repeat the words of Patton for all to hear: Thank God such men as Pat Tillman lived.

---

5. "Harvey Araton, "An Exception in an Age of Celebrity," *The New York Times*, Apr. 24, 2004.

CHAPTER 35

No Greater Love:
The Life and Death of Michael Monsoor

BY NORMAN FULKERSON

Representative characters see themselves as connected to society. They are not just extraordinary individuals. They maintain ties to those whom they love. They step up to the plate and sacrifice themselves for others, even to the point of giving their lives. Such examples inspire society and lead others to admire and imitate them. Without such examples, people become mired in their own interests and all society suffers as a result.

On September 29, 2006, Ramadi, Iraq was considered the most dangerous city on planet earth for American servicemen. Michael Monsoor was there in the midst of it all. He was a member of the elite branch of the Navy called SEALs, which stands for SEa, Air, and Land. On that day, he was on a rooftop overwatch in the most contested part of the city, called the Ma'laab district.

Positioned near the only exit, with an Mk 48 machine gun in hand, he was providing security for two SEAL snipers who lay in prone positions on either side of him. Moments later a fragmentation grenade bounced off his chest and landed on the ground....

Becoming a Navy SEAL

Although nothing can adequately prepare one for such a circumstance, Michael Monsoor seemed to be living a life which pointed to it. He was an adventuresome boy growing up in Southern California. His father, George, and older brother, Jim, had both been proud Marines. His boyhood dream of being a SEAL began to be realized when, at 20 years of age, he joined the Navy.

In the first phase of training, he broke his heel. Exhibiting the selflessness which would become his trademark, he continued to run with a pain so excruciating he nearly passed out. Unable to continue, he was forced to ring the bell indicating that a trainee had quit the program.

He was medically rolled back and sent to Italy for a year where he spent the majority of his off time doing physical training. His mother, Sally, when visiting him, said he hardly ever stopped running.

He then reentered a grueling SEAL program where only 23 percent pass, graduated at the top in the class of 2005, and was assigned to Delta Platoon. In April 2006 he was sent to Iraq on his first tour of duty.

From here we almost lose our breath as we follow the rapid upward trajectory his life would take.

Rescued from the Jaws of Death

As a heavy weapons machine gunner, his position while patrolling the streets of Ramadi with Delta Company was right behind the point man. The responsibility for protecting the rest of the unit fell squarely on his shoulders. It was an appropriate position for a Catholic young man named after the warrior angel, Saint Michael.

He was also a SEAL communicator, which required him to carry a

rucksack full of communications equipment in addition to his Mk 48 machine gun full of ammunition. He carried the extra 100 lbs. without complaint, in temperatures as high as 130 degrees.

In May of 2006, during his first month in Iraq, his unit came under fire during counter-terrorist operations. Heavy enemy automatic weapons fire resulted in a wounded SEAL who was left exposed to enemy fire. Michael threw caution to the wind and ran directly into the line of fire to help the injured soldier. As gunfire chewed up the asphalt around him, Michael snatched the wounded soldier from the

Michael Monsoor was always in the center of the battle.

jaws of death with one arm, returned enemy fire with the other, and then dragged him to safety.

He then maintained suppressive fire while the wounded SEAL received tactical casualty treatment. After loading his wounded teammate onto an evacuation vehicle, he returned to the battle. This act of heroism earned him a Silver Star and a reputation for putting others first.

Some months later the injured soldier had a dream of the incident where the Michael who rescued him had wings. He later had an artist make a reproduction of the image in his dream, depicting Michael Monsoor in dress blues with a loaded Mk 48 Machine gun and silvery wings. As a tribute to Saint Michael the Archangel, who he felt was there with them, he included the short exorcism which invokes the warrior angel to "be our protection against wickedness."

Streets Paved with Fire

Such protection was sorely needed, especially considering that 75 percent of the missions involving Michael's platoon came under attack. Thirty-five escalated into heated firefights taking place in "streets that were paved with fire."[1]

During eleven of those missions, Michael's leadership, guidance, and decisive action were key in saving the lives of many of his men. For his heroism, he was awarded the Bronze Star. The citation accompanying the medal describes how he "exposed himself to heavy enemy fire while shielding his teammates with suppressive fire. He aggressively stabilized each chaotic situation with focused determination and uncanny tactical awareness. Each time [terrorists] assaulted his team with small arms fire or rocket-propelled grenades, he quickly assessed the situation, determined the best course of action to counter the enemy assaults, and implemented his plan to gain the best tactical advantage."[2]

In the midst of such violent action, Michael Monsoor displayed what Secretary of the Navy, Donald Winter, described as a "cool-headedness under fire" and "when hostility broke out, he proved he was a SEAL you wanted on your team."[3]

As extraordinary as all of this is, it was merely a prelude to the defining moment of his life in the rooftop overwatch.

"Path of Honor"

When the grenade landed in front of him, Michael Monsoor knew that the length of the fuse would not allow him to toss it out. He also knew that he was two short weeks away from returning home to family and

---

1. U.S. Navy Seal Mike Monsoor—Awarded the Medal of Honor," Apr. 7, 2008, accessed Jun. 7, 2017, http://www.blackfive.net/main/2008/04/us-navy-seal-mi.html.

2. http://www.navy.mil/moh/Monsoor/bronze.pdf.

3. http://www.navy.mil/moh/Monsoor/hoh.html.

friends. Plans were already made for him to see his younger brother play in a football game for North Dakota's Minot State University.[4]

With the only exit door at his back, a live grenade at his feet, and two Navy Seals in front of him, he was faced with the hardest decision of his life. It was one of those rare moments when life passes before your eyes. Having already endured so many hardships and numerous brushes with death, no one would have faulted him had he chosen a path to safety.

"He chose a different path," said Mr. Winter, "a path of honor." On numerous occasions, Michael Monsoor stared death in the face in his heroic defense of others. Once again he and death would meet, and once again he put others first. With unflinching selflessness, he gave his life so that others might live. In so doing, he saved the lives of three Navy SEALs and eight Iraqi soldiers.

One of the survivors described how "Mikey" looked death in the face that day and said, "You cannot take my brothers, I will go in their stead."[5]

"He never took his eye off the grenade, his only movement was down and toward it," said a 28-year-old lieutenant who lived to tell the story. "He undoubtedly saved mine and the other SEALs' lives."[6]

Another eyewitness described Michael's countenance as "completely calm, showing no fear, only resolve."

It could easily be said of him what Gen. Pericles said in his funeral oration for the warriors of ancient Athens: "He passed away from the scene, not of his fear, but of his glory."

Feast of Saint Michael the Archangel

Michael Monsoor was immediately evacuated to a battalion aid station. Fr. Paul Anthony Halladay, his platoon chaplain, was with Michael as he passed away approximately 30 minutes later.

It was an appropriate end for a Catholic soldier who, according to many reports, was a practicing Catholic. His fellow soldiers told how

---

4. http://www.landstuhlhospitalcareproject.org/Honorees/Michael%20A.%20Monsoor/Michael%20A.%20Monsoor.html.

5. http://mksviews.wordpress.com/2008/04/23/you-cannot-take-my-brothers-i-will-go-in-their-stead.

6. "Navy SEAL Dies Saving Comrades," Oct. 14, 2006, accessed Jun. 7, 2017, http://www.military.com/NewsContent/0,13319,116817,00.html.

he frequently attended mass "with devotion" before his operations.

Patricia Monsoor, his aunt and godmother, said he "went to confession frequently" and "other soldiers who were not practicing would sometimes follow [him to Mass] because of his good example."

When he was posthumously awarded the Medal of Honor, a tearful President Bush reminded the audience that the day Michael Monsoor died was the feast of Saint Michael the Archangel.

An emotional Donald Winter quoted a passage from scripture already remembered by so many to describe Michael Monsoor: "Greater love than this no man hath, that a man lay down his life for his friends."

"When it came down to laying down his life for his friends, his faith allowed him to [do so] without a moment's hesitation," said Father Halladay.[7]

"I Have Given Everything"

The most moving tribute to Petty Officer Michael Monsoor was that given by Lieutenant Commander John Willink during an evening ceremony at the Navy Memorial honoring the fallen hero.[8]

He described in detail a photo of Michael released shortly after his death. The picture shows Michael walking at the head of his platoon, through the war-torn streets of Ramadi. They are shrouded in a greenish yellow mist used to mask their movements from the enemy. In spite of the chaos and danger which surrounds them, Michael is calm, almost smiling.

"As I look at this picture," Lt. Cdr. Willink said, "I hear a voice in a humble but confident tone."

He then finishes his speech with the words he imagines Michael saying to him. They are words which I feel Michael Monsoor is saying to every American who appreciates the unbelievable sacrifice he made in a faraway land, far from his family and the country he loved.

"'I am Michael Monsoor....I am patrolling the streets of Ramadi.... My eyes sting from the sweat, my gun and gear are heavy, but these things do not bother me. There is no comfort here, but this is the life I have chosen, and there is no place I would rather be...and I am ready.

"'I am Michael Monsoor....I miss my family. I want to hold my nieces

---

7. "Michael Anthony Monsoor Story," *Catholic News Service*, Apr. 11, 2008, accessed Jun. 7, 2017, http://www.freerepublic.com/focus/religion/2006608/posts?page=5.

8. http://www.navy.mil/moh/Monsoor/flag.html.

and nephews again. I want to make them smile and laugh, but I am far from home. Instead, I smile at the Iraqi children when we pass them by. When we encounter Iraqi families, I treat them with respect and dignity. I know the importance of family because there is nothing more important to me than my family....

"'I am Michael Monsoor, I love my country, my fellow SEALs, and the men fighting alongside us....I have lived life to its fullest. I have not looked back. I leave nothing but love, and I have no regrets.

"'I am Michael Monsoor...and I have given everything...for you!'"

CHAPTER 36

True Valor Is Priceless

BY NORMAN FULKERSON

Representative characters are those who lead by their example and determination. They do not allow themselves to be limited by what seems to be overwhelming odds. They embrace the odds and the crosses that stand in their way and overcome them. Indeed, every family or association could have "legendary" members that, by their extraordinary deeds, perfections, or works, would elevate the whole family or group. Their feats would then be told and retold to succeeding generations.

When Michael Monsoor jumped on a grenade to save the lives of three Navy SEALs in September of 2006, the nation was left speechless. The Medal of Honor was presented to his grieving parents during a White House reception, as a mournful audience looked on. There was a man in the room that day that might have seemed like just another soldier, if not for the peculiar spring in his step.

His name is William "Spanky" Gibson. He had just flown in from overseas and had a good reason for being present at the ceremony. He had lost his left leg during a firefight in Iraq six months before, and it was the cover Michael Monsoor provided from a rooftop overlook that contributed toward saving his life. It would be hard to find someone more worthy of that sacrifice than William Gibson. Like Petty Officer Monsoor, he is a tribute to the American soldier, and his story deserves to be told.

Gunnery Seargent William "Spanky" Gibson

Idealistic Youth

William Gibson acquired the nickname "Spanky" in boot camp. Although it had nothing to do with his likeness to the round-faced kid in The Little Rascals series, he does radiate much of the innocent charm of that little boy.

By the time "Spanky" was only five years old, his father, William Sr., said he knew exactly what he wanted to be in life. "When I grow up," he said, "I am going to be just like grandpa."

His grandfather, Peterson Parrott, a 30-year Marine, visited his impressionable grandson on a stopover while transferring from the East to the West coast. When Spanky saw his grandfather in uniform with all his decorations, he was fascinated. During his stay, Mr. Parrott kept his medals on a high shelf out of reach of the idealistic youth, but made him a promise: "When you grow tall enough to reach those medals," Mr. Parrott said, "You can have them."

By the time he grew tall enough, he had already joined the Marines and was well on his way to earning his own medals for bravery. "[A soldier is] all he ever wanted to be," said his father.

Firefight in Ramadi

Shortly after joining the Marine Corps, he earned the rank of gunnery sergeant. In May of 2006, he was leading a four-man team through the streets of Ramadi, Iraq, on a foot patrol. They were searching for the notorious Abu Musab al-Zarqawi in the most dangerous city on earth.

Alongside him was an Iraqi soldier; a man he had helped train. Suddenly they came under fire from a sniper in a nearby house. The Iraqi soldier was shot in the knee and incapacitated. With total disregard for his safety, Sgt. Gibson was running to his rescue when a 30-caliber round ripped through his left knee cap, destroying the socket and severing his femoral artery.

The identical nature of the injuries, coming from a trained enemy marksman, might have been an intentional plan to increase the confusion of an already violent firefight. If they thought Sgt. Gibson would just lie there screaming in pain before being finished off later, they were sorely mistaken.

"Gunny" Gibson, as his men often called him, never missed a beat. Thinking that his knee had only given out, he attempted to stand before realizing the severity of his injury. Not allowing this to deter him, he simply rolled over and began returning fire. If not for the immediate assistance given to him by a SEAL corpsman, he would have bled to death on the battlefield. As he was dragged from the scene, he continued to lay down suppressive fire in spite of the pain and massive loss of blood.

"When Can I Return to Iraq?"

When Sgt. Gibson was eventually flown back to the United States, waiting for him at the airport was Gen. Michael Hagee, the Commandant of the Marine Corps. Without a trace of self-pity, Sgt. Gibson asked the Commandant a curious question: "What will this do to my career?"

The Commandant assured him that it would affect his career only to the degree that he allowed it to do so. This was a veritable invitation for Sgt. Gibson to fight as hard towards full rehabilitation as he fought on the streets of Ramadi. The fight began when he was encouraged to get out of the Marine Corps. Undeterred by the suggestion, William Gibson called the Commandant directly and found the support he needed to remain.

What Sgt. Gibson faced later is truly inspiring. The lower part of his left leg had been amputated overseas before he arrived at Bethesda Naval Hospital in Maryland. In spite of the seriousness of his injury, he mystified those around him with the constant inquiry: "When can I return to Iraq?"

Those witnessing such determination were shocked, considering he might lose the rest of his leg. They were wondering how he would adjust to life with a prosthetic leg while Sgt. Gibson was thinking about fighting a war with one.

"I would beg the surgeons every time they would come in," he said with a smile, "to cut it off, close me up and get me out of here."[1]

He knew that "out of here" meant one step closer to his goal of returning to combat with or without the remaining part of his left leg. The surgeons were unsuccessful. Sgt. Gibson ended up losing the rest of his leg, but he never lost his will to fight.

"It isn't growing back" he was quoted as saying, "so let's start recovering."[2]

As unbelievable as this might be, Sgt. Gibson's attitude towards a

---

1. "Mike Monsoor and Spanky Gibson," *Soldiers' Angels Germany*, Apr. 11, 2008, accessed Jun. 7, 2017, http://soldiersangelsgermany.blogspot.com/2008/04/mike-monsoor-and-spanky-gibson.html.

2. Jennifer Griffin, "Iraq War Veteran with Amputated Leg Back on Active Duty," Feb. 29, 2008, accessed Jun. 7, 2017, http://www.foxnews.com/story/0,2933,333534,00.html.

long recovery was even more so: "What is the shortest time of anyone recovering from such an injury?" his wife Chaney remembered him asking the doctors. He was told that the quickest anyone made it through rehab was thirteen months, but some were as long as eighteen to twenty-four months.

"I am not doing that," was Sgt. Gibson defiant response.

Escape from Alcatraz

He then began an astonishing rehabilitation program. Two months after his injury he stopped taking all his medicine, including that for pain, so as to be clearheaded and focused.

Sgt. Gibson finishes the Marine Corps Marathon 10k.

Shortly after that, he began taking his first steps on a new prosthetic leg with the help of crutches. Three months later, he participated in the Marine Corps Marathon, and then it was on to skiing and later ice climbing.

It wasn't long before he tackled something which even a man with two legs would hesitate attempting: the Escape from Alcatraz Triathlon. This would turn out to be the break he needed to return to Iraq.

The Triathlon is a yearly event in which swimmers are dropped on the island in the San Francisco Bay where the famous prison is located. The first part of the Triathlon entails swimming to shore in freezing-cold, shark-infested waters. Sgt. Gibson made the swim with only one leg and came in among the top ten.

When he reached the shore, he was greeted by the Commander of the 1st Marine Expeditionary Force, General James Mattis. "What can I do for you, Marine?" Gen. Mattis asked the winded but determined soldier.

"I want to be re-deployed," said Sgt. Gibson.

"You can come with me in January," Gen. Mattis said, "or a later flight. Which would you prefer?"

Sgt. Gibson chose the first flight out, and after making the trip in

January of 2008 with General James Mattis, he has become the first full leg amputee ever to return to duty in a combat zone.

"I Have Just Done My Job"

Although what he has done is extraordinary, his mother says her son wouldn't agree. "He doesn't feel like he has done anything special," she says. In the face of a writer who approached the family with the idea of writing a book about Sgt. Gibson, his mother says his attitude remained the same. "Why would anyone want to read about me?" he argues, "I have just done my job."

Perhaps the most amazing thing about William Gibson is his refusal to allow the loss of a leg to get him down. This, no doubt, is a character trait he inherited from his father, a Vietnam veteran who suffered a broken back in combat. When doctors told William Sr. that he would never walk again, he proved them wrong. "You never say 'can't,'" Mr. Gibson said. "It might be difficult, but you can do it."

The only moment of sadness for Sgt. Gibson came with the thought of having to leave the battlefield after his injury. Chaney Gibson described her husband as someone who leads by example. "He would never put one of his Marines out there alone to get hurt," she said. "He felt like he had to protect them."

At the time he was wounded, Sgt. Gibson was a 35-year-old veteran Marine, fighting alongside much younger Marines who were seeing their first action. He believed firmly in leading his men in battle, not pushing them from behind. It was for this reason that he was disappointed at having to leave "his boys" alone in combat while he was evacuated.

He would go on to say that if given a chance to change anything that happened that day, he wouldn't. "Better me," he said, "than one of my men."

* * *

Sgt. Gibson back in uniform.

Sgt. William "Spanky" Gibson is safely home now, and while his return to battle without a leg might have earned him a place in the history books, his example has earned him a place in the heart of every patriotic American. He represents all the best our country has to offer, and it is nice to know that the sniper bullet which cost him a leg didn't touch his honor. Bullets, after all, can be purchased, but true valor is priceless.

CHAPTER 37

Where Are the Nation's Captains?

BY JOHN HORVAT II

Representative characters appear in times of crisis. They take upon themselves the task of leading. Most people think leading means simply giving orders. Leading involves much more. Rather, true leaders must have a connection with those who follow them. They must be on the scene, appearing, reassuring, and orienting those under them. This means being visibly in charge of the situation so that by their actions, they can take a group of many people and unite them as one, to accomplish a common goal.

Traveling by air these days can be stressful. It is increasingly difficult to go on a trip without some incident happening. More often, however, flights are canceled or delayed due to mechanical or weather problems. This can lead to hours of waiting at the gates, compounded by the constant uncertainty about what is going on. However, enduring these incidents can be a real lesson about society in general.

I experienced two flights during a recent trip that displayed opposite ways of dealing with problems. It got me thinking about what is needed in times of crises on a larger scale.

A Slight Delay Becomes a Nightmare

The first incident was a short one-hour flight that would generally present few problems. This particular six o'clock flight was due to arrive at its destination at seven. The trouble began with a short half-hour delay. Apparently, there was a small mechanical problem that needed to be fixed and would only take a short while to remedy.

The short while soon became a long delay as problems compounded. One hour, two hours, three hours passed. Waiting is always difficult, but the worst thing was the unknown. No one seemed to know what was going on, or at least would not tell us. We were left in the dark. The personnel at the desk, although polite, were hardly reassuring.

The situation started to get ugly when the captain and crew inexplicably walked out of the plane and left the scene. We did not know why they left, but later figured out they had timed out their hours and by law could not fly. It was later announced that another plane had been found and that all were instructed to scramble over to another gate in the next terminal.

There was no plane at the next terminal. Passengers started to get angry and confront the poor airline representative left at the desk. People began to make problems and create scenes. No one seemed to be in charge. A plane finally arrived, but then we were told that the pilots and crew had been called to the airport and would not make it in for another hour. After a time of chaos and confusion, the plane took off after midnight. An hour later, we landed, and our nightmare was over.

A Similar Situation Develops

I would have typically dismissed the incident as just another misadventure that has become part of traveling in these times. However, my next flight a few days later provided such a marked contrast that it helped me see a larger picture.

On this second occasion, the three-hour flight was slightly delayed because of weather problems. However, we soon boarded the plane, and everyone took their seats. We were all ready to leave the gate when the captain announced that there would be a delay because the tower at the destination would not give him permission to land.

Such an announcement hardly pleased the passengers that were cooped up in the plane. Everyone started to get a bit edgy with the news and the prospect of spending an hour or more at the gate—but then something unexpected happened, something that astonished me.

A Commanding Presence Reassures

As I looked down the aisle, I saw the figure of the captain. He was slowly making his way to the back of the plane explaining to everyone what was happening. He would stop and answer any questions and reassure everyone that he was doing his best to get this plane in the air. He was clearly in charge.

After returning to the cockpit, everyone waited. The pilot then made another announcement that the plane would be even further delayed. For a second time, he went down the aisle answering questions and reassuring passengers. The atmosphere aboard the plane was calm. People were not upset or angry. The captain's prompt actions and commanding presence put them all at ease.

The captain later made an announcement that by law everyone had to leave the cabin and stretch their legs, which everyone considered absurd. He apologized for the inconvenience, yet firmly insisted that all comply. Everyone left without problems or complaint.

Finally, we took off, and the plane landed without incident. As I was leaving the plane, I could not resist asking one of the stewardesses if the captain's going down the aisle was airline policy. She replied that it was not, but it was the way this particular captain operated. "Everyone likes to work with him. We love him," she concluded.

A Tale of Two Flights

The contrast between the two incidents could not be more glaring. Here were two crisis situations that demanded leadership. In the first instance, no one seemed to care as long as all protocol was being followed. In the second case, everyone felt reassured that the situation was under control. The first flight had a pilot; the second had a captain.

The captain's job is not merely to fly the plane. His role is to coordinate and harmonize the flight, dealing with whatever problems might arise, and deliver his passengers safely to the destination. The captain must connect with those under him and reassure them.

Searching for Captains

I cannot help but think that society is missing many captains today. So many go about the business of piloting and doing what is technically correct. They stay in their cockpits, so to speak, performing the task at hand. They do not go the extra mile to reassure those desperately looking for direction. Too few want to assume the responsibility of showing themselves in authority—for fear of offending others by asking people to do what they might not want to do.

We need captains everywhere today. They are sadly lacking in the family, schools, industry, politics, and religion. This is largely because people do not have a proper notion of what captains are. They think authority consists only in ordering people to do things. They do not realize that it also involves unifying, reassuring, and harmonizing.

Saint Thomas Aquinas defines authority as an animating and ordering intelligence, the *vis regitiva*, that overcomes the resistance of the individual tendencies in men, organically directing and coordinating many wills toward the common good.

Thus, captains respect order and do not violate the rules, however difficult or absurd such rules might appear to others. Captains do not pander to those under them to please them. They do not make grand promises, yet fail to mention the sacrifices needed to get the job done. Captains recognize that people need direction and act accordingly.

Above all, captains need to connect with those working with them to distil the best from them. Contrary to our egalitarian times, captains are not just "ordinary guys." They need to appear as key representative figures, visibly and reassuringly, so as to secure the cooperation and confidence of those under them. Captains selflessly dedicate themselves to defending the common good to the point that they sacrifice themselves for and serve those whom they command.

Indeed, in our confusing and chaotic times, we do not need technocrats, economists, and politicians to craft their complex programs to solve our problems. We need to ask: Where are the nation's captains?

CHAPTER 38

The Passing of a King

BY JOHN HORVAT II

Representative characters involve statesmen and political leaders. They hold offices that require them to think in terms of the common good. Thus, real political leaders need to be especially careful not to put their own interest above that of those they serve. Rather they should hold themselves to high standards. When they possess virtues, they can do an enormous amount of good and earn the respect of the people.

I would see him from time to time at Catholic events and meetings in Washington, D.C. He was a seven-foot-tall African gentleman who was always very courteous and soft-spoken. He had a stately bearing that was at the same time dignified and disarming. I am told he was very pious and could often be seen at Mass or with a rosary in his hand. He commanded respect, but it was not difficult to walk up and converse with him. A couple of times, I had the honor of speaking with the king.

Indeed, he was a king, a Catholic king who was, in fact, the last anointed African king living. It was with great sadness that I heard the news of the death of King Kigeli V of Rwanda, 80, who passed away at a Washington-area hospital.

The news set the stage for some reflections. I reflected upon how his life was one of turmoil and suffering, which he bore well. He became king in the turbulent times of African independence when revolutionary liberation movements were wreaking havoc on the continent.

King Kigeli V of Rwanda.

Rwanda was not exempt from the unrest. Just before independence, ethnic rivalry led to the forced exiling of many Tutsi tribal people. The departing Belgian administrators added to the confusion by arranging King Kigeli's exile in 1961. This was followed by the typical succession of "democratic" African governments that culminated in the 1994 wave of anarchy and mass killings in which as many as a half-million civilians, mostly Tutsi, were slaughtered.

In exile, the king did not lead an ordinary life. He respected the Rwandan tradition that an exiled king does not marry and thus remained single. Most of his time in exile was spent helping Rwandan refugees. Foremost in his mind was working toward the unity of his suffering people.

What impressed me about the king was that you sensed he was sincere and authentic. He was not a politician who was looking to build a career. Deprived of his considerable wealth in Rwanda, he lived humbly and had nothing to gain by advocating the cause of his people.

He was what sociologists call a "representative character." Noted philosopher Alasdair MacIntyre wrote that such characters "are, so to speak, the moral representatives of their culture and they are so because of the way in which moral and metaphysical ideas and theories assume through them an embodied existence in the social world."

These figures exist in every society, including our own. No one elects them. They are natural leaders who can take the principles, moral qualities, and virtues desired and needed by their communities and translate them into concrete programs of life and culture.

There is no doubt in my mind that the king was one of these unassuming representative characters. He was truly a moral representative of his culture. This was recognized by many Rwandans who asked that he be allowed to return and even serve as a unifying figure in the fragmented central African nation.

The history of his life is very important, but it was not these details that struck me upon hearing the news of his death. The passing of King Kigeli V was a tragic reminder of how far we as a nation have descended.

I remember seeing the king with his calm demeanor and dignity sitting in an armchair. Reflecting upon this scene, I cannot help but think about how I, as an American, somehow feel much more represented by this foreign figure than American counterparts. King Kigeli personified so many of the qualities missing in today's political discourse: honor, dignity, longsuffering, piety, and self-sacrifice. The contrast between this tall African gentleman and the present political figures could not be more striking.

Everyone senses this difference when comparing our past and current standards of political behavior. No one is happy with the situation.

Looking at the political scene, so many Americans are experiencing frustration, exasperation, and anxiety at what is happening.

It used to be that public figures addressed each other politely. Courtesy and civility were considered political virtues, not weaknesses to be exploited. Candidates did not engage in dishonorable lying or promiscuous personal conduct. People used to feel *they could be represented* by the figures presented to them.

Today, all that has changed. The change is part of the political culture of both parties varying only in degree. Everything has become so brutal and frenzied. There is no longer thoughtful debate, but rather programmed sound bites and tailored tweets to attract the attention of the distracted masses. We have turned the election into a political wrestling match, no holds barred.

Instead of the representative characters, we now have *unrepresentative* characters who do not represent what we want to be. We brought ourselves to this point by embracing a culture of frenetic intemperance in which everyone wants everything instantly and effortlessly. Lifestyles of gratification and self-centeredness bring out the worst in us. All this is tearing our society and economy apart. We see it affecting the political process.

This culture is imploding. It is unsustainable and weighs heavily upon the land. Its chaotic discourse tires us out and awakens in us longings for a return to order. When the disorder reaches its climax, and things come crashing down, it is important that there be figures like the king who will remind us of what we have left behind. Then we will look for those representative characters that represent that which is still good in America. The qualities found in good King Kigeli V (and needed by so many of our elected officials) will again be appreciated and valued.

In the meantime, let all who read this say a prayer for the repose of the soul of the pious Catholic king. May God grant him eternal rest. Even in death, he showed magnanimity. At the time of his funeral, those wishing to donate to help defray the expenses were advised by the King's website to consider applying them first to "educational institutions that support Rwandan students in His Majesty's name."

PART V

WHEN MEN DREAM

Any return to order cannot consist of only a material restoration of the past. The primary element must consist of awakening in ourselves great desires for those sublime things that lift us up from the daily concerns of our lives. Such spiritual desires set our dreams in motion. When men dream, marvelous things happen. Civilizations flourish. Legends are born.

By "dream" we mean the process by which we idealize our goals in society. There comes a time when individuals and families unite to form a consensus about how they might make their lives more perfect. They then conceive new ways of expressing and manifesting themselves in line with these desires. Thus families, social units, or peoples envision a future for themselves that considers both the practical means at hand and a higher ideal. They begin to consider those things that are on the limits of what is possible.

"Without the metaphysical dream it is impossible to think of men living together harmoniously over an extent of time," writes Richard Weaver. "The dream carries with it an evaluation, which is the bond of spiritual community."

This section will feature stories that narrate the dreams of those who envisioned a more perfect life and expressed it through great works, practices, or even products.

As can be seen from the examples we will be sharing, these dreams need not be extremely elaborate. The people involved need not be rich or talented. They must have the courage to ask, "What if?" and the fortitude to carry their projects to completion. Above all, dreams require admiring hearts that seek out the good, true, and beautiful, wherever it might be found. Dreams create conditions to unify peoples and for representative characters to appear.

We need to point out that this desire for the dream that so attracts modern man ultimately leads to God. It is ironic that in our materialistic and secular age, we find a great thirst for God and the supernatural. This type of dream, sustained by grace, is what the Church proposed and spread throughout Christendom. It is what Prof. Plinio Corrêa de Oliveira called the "most striking, indisputable, and audacious dream imaginable."

The great desire for sublime ideals through the workings of grace is an essential component of any return to order.

Longwood Gardens, "A Little Piece of Heaven"

BY NORMAN FULKERSON

When men dream, they begin exploring what is seemingly impossible. They are always asking: What if we do this? For this reason, they are always seeking out beauty, and desire to share this beauty so that others might also admire God's creation. Sometimes this quest becomes a pursuit of a lifetime and extends to future generations. Such is the case of Longwood Gardens, a dream come true for one family and now the delight of a public attracted to this marvelous wonder.

The facts are staggering. Here you will find the greatest and the most in nearly every conceivable category: 1,050 acres of gardens containing exquisite flowers and majestic trees, twenty different outdoor gardens, twenty indoor gardens in four acres of heated greenhouses, and a total of 11,000 different species of plants, all making this one of the greatest conservatories in the world.

In addition to the plants, there are dazzling fountains with variable multi-colored illumination, musical accompaniment, and a backdrop of fireworks on selected summer evenings, a spectacle that leaves the attendees spellbound. Then there are the over 800 horticultural and performing arts events ranging from flower shows, horticultural classes, and children's programs to concerts, organ recitals, and musical plays. Finally, there is the impressive tally of over 900,000 people entering the gates each year.

Reducing this world of variety to its least common denominator, we find that all of this is the dream of one man, Pierre Samuel du Pont (1870–1954). In a country where the majority rules, one man put together a garden that has enchanted people for decades. Only in America!

Pierre was the great-grandson of Eleuthère Irénée du Pont (1771–1834), a royalist who left France in 1800 and founded the family fortune by manufacturing gunpowder. Pierre later turned the family business into a chemical corporate empire. Using his wealth and his leisure, Pierre developed what was to become Longwood Gardens. The inspiration for Longwood came from his numerous trips to Europe, where

Longwood Gardens, a true marvel open to the public.

he visited some two dozen villas and fifty chateaux. He even visited the garden of Claude Oscar Monet, hosted by the painter himself.

He threw himself into his projects with an unbounded energy. At 21 years of age, he oversaw the construction of the new family homestead. By the time he was 28, he possessed his own commercial nursery with seven greenhouses. At 34, disappointed by professional landscapers, he drafted his own plans for improving the family's estate. He began work on what is known today as Longwood Gardens at the age of 36, starting with the 600-foot long Flower Garden Walk in 1907, and continued to build as the "mood touched him." At his urging, the Longwood Foundation was established in 1946, entrusted to operate the gardens "for the sole use of the public for purposes of exhibition, instruction, education, and enjoyment."

While visiting Longwood, I spoke with Mr. Colvin Randall, its Public Relations Manager. One of the first things I asked was whether any descendants of Pierre were still involved in the foundation. "Du Ponts were involved in the beginning of this foundation and are still involved in the running of Longwood," he said. "Two-thirds of the board of trustees is made up of family members. Mr. du Pont didn't have any children, so they are mostly his great-nephews and great-nieces, and a few of them carry the name du Pont."

"Do they have horticultural experience?" I asked. "They are well known and respected in botanical circles," Mr. Randall replied. "They are primarily responsible, in addition to the financial end of Longwood, for the aesthetical questions of taste. They decide what is tasteful and what is not. They meet once a month with the advisory committee and the landscape committee and review design changes for the garden. These are things like color combinations, any buildings to be built, the details, or the architectural styles. It always goes through these trustees' committees."

That eye for the tasteful, which runs in the du Pont family, is the soul of Longwood Gardens. It is something that goes beyond mere botany and touches the sublime. It was ultimately the fruit of a little boy's dream. When Pierre was only nine, he visited a mansion in Philadelphia which had a conservatory. "If one day I ever build a green-house," he said, "it will be open to the public."

In this innocent dream, he not only yearned for beautiful things, but desired to share them with others. Much later, visiting Florence with his wife, he marveled at the Villa Gamberaia water garden, exclaiming, "Wouldn't it be nice to have this in the United States?" Eventually, a re-production of this beautiful Italian water garden, with several en-hancements of Pierre's own design, was added near one of Longwood's shaded paths, permitting visitors to share his earlier delight. Following the direction of his dream, Mr. du Pont continued his quest for a gar-den of ever-greater beauty and quality. With the establishment of the foundation and the continual influence of members of the du Pont family, his dream continues. The success of Longwood Gardens is proof of its appeal.

Attaining high ideals, the fruit of a healthy tradition, however, has a value too few seem to realize in today's world. All too many people are caught up in matters that fail to capture the imagination. Tax breaks, Wall Street trends, and healthcare are all problems that must be ad-dressed, but they are not the stuff from which dreams are made. What people need are ideals to believe in, to strive for. It is part of our nature, it is what drives us to succeed and go forward, giving that spice and zest which life otherwise lacks. Ultimately, it is this love for the dream that gives people the energy and enthusiasm to go the extra mile and achieve things so great that those who lack the dream can only sit back and wonder.

This idea is expressed very well in an advertisement showing a man clinging to the side of a cliff, clutching at any little crack in the rock that would allow him to go higher. The caption is simple: "My body was not made for this, but my spirit was." Although the ideal dream is not based on the thrills and sensations that are so prevalent in our modern world, it does generate this effect in man. It gives him a vitality of spirit and the necessary drive to accomplish that which his mere natural strength would not be able to do. This explains the attitudes of the people one meets while visiting Longwood.

One enthusiastic visitor from New York, for example, realizing that I was visiting the gardens for the first time, exclaimed with a gleam in her eye how she had visited many times and always found something new to "ooh and ah about." The joy in her eyes while expressing her enthusiasm for the gardens was contagious. Then there were the four ladies who walked single file into a hall adorned with hanging globes of pink chrysanthemums. "Oh, my heavens!" each exclaimed in turn upon entering the hall. The last lady expressed what all three probably thought: "Did you ever see anything more beautiful in your life?"

It is truly impossible to visit Longwood as a passive observer. Everyone is quickly absorbed by the grandeur of it all. Walking along the finely manicured lawns, seeing the play of lights in the hundreds of fountains, is a dream. An atmosphere of joy and innocence envelops everyone, old and young, men, women, and children, all enjoying the fruits of Pierre's labors, the fulfillment of his dreams.

The combination of fountains, lights and gardens is overwhelming.

One little boy put it best when he exclaimed, "Oh, this is just like a little piece of heaven." This boy realized in his innocence what few adults are ever able to grasp. He saw exactly that which another little boy in Philadelphia was dreaming of many years before him: a heavenly garden made for people's enjoyment. Finally, there was the comment someone wrote in a survey put out by Longwood: "What would God do if He had money?"

This question begs an answer, and it is very simple: God would do exactly that which He inspires His creatures to do when they are faithful to their dreams.

CHAPTER 40

The Reigning Monarch of Instruments
BY NORMAN FULKERSON

Dreams can start with one person and be carried on by others. In the search for the sublime, many are suddenly called and give of themselves selflessly so that others might also share the dream. Such is the case of the Wanamaker organ, the grandest of grand organs and the largest musical instrument in the world.

Moreau Claude, an organist from Paris, appreciates such things. After all, he has a beautiful organ in his home and has studied under Marcel Dupré. For his 70th birthday, his daughter bought him a ticket to see this grand organ and fulfill his lifelong dream. It was a round-trip international ticket, however, since this instrument's home is not in Europe, but in the Lord and Taylor department store in downtown Philadelphia.

After hearing the organ play on Monday and Tuesday, a happy Mr. Claude and his daughter got back on the plane Wednesday for the long trip home. According to the official organist, Peter Conte, such trips are not uncommon. "There are other people in Europe," he said, "that save up for years to come over and see it." Such trips he referred to as veritable pilgrimages.

It seemed odd to me that such a thing would exist in a department store. That is the reason I had to see it for myself. As I walked through the doors and past the men's clothing area, I arrived at the Grand Court which is 112 feet long and 66 feet wide.

Expecting merely to hear an instrument of excellent quality, my first thought upon seeing this organ was how stunningly beautiful it was. Its golden

The Wannamaker is the largest musical instrument in the world.

hue and multilayer structuring emit a defined sense of hierarchy synonymous with queenly dignity. I felt I was indeed being received in audience by something a brochure I picked up aptly defined as "The Reigning Monarch of Instruments." Her throne is appropriately located high above the gallery on the south end of the court; a gallery which seats 100 musicians on special occasions.

History of the Wanamaker

The history of this organ is as rich as her regal surroundings. In the late 1800s, a man by the name of John Wanamaker opened a "new kind of store." It was to be a place where you could buy just about everything under one roof. It was said in those days that "if you couldn't buy it at Wanamaker's, you couldn't get it in Philadelphia."

The Console

The present console was built in the late 1920s and installed between

1930 and 1932. It controls the Grand Court Organ and, with a total weight of 5,800 pounds, contains approximately 100,000 parts. It has 729 tilting tablets, 168 pistons, and 55 auxiliary controls. It stands on a pivot and truck to facilitate rotation.

One thing Mr. Wanamaker lacked, however, was an organ for the entertainment of his customers. He believed music was just as important to a well-rounded life as work and exercise. He thus began a trend, which became common in the early 1900s, for department stores to provide soothing organ music for their shoppers.

Peter Conte considered this practice to be a continuation of an English tradition of having an organ in a central public space. "In those days, they couldn't afford an orchestra," he said, "so the organist became a one-man band who would play transcriptions of everyone's favorite orchestral music."

The present console controls the Grand Court Organ and, with a total weight of 5800 pounds, contains approximately 100,000 parts. It has 729 tilting tablets, 168 pistons and 55 auxiliary controls.

© Tneorg | Dreamstime.com

A New Acquisition for the Wanamaker Store

So it was that John Wanamaker's son Rodman bought the famous Louisiana Purchase Organ now known simply as the Wanamaker. It had been displayed at the 1904 St. Louis World's Fair and was sitting in a warehouse after plans for installing it in the Kansas City Municipal Auditorium fell through.

After being transported to Philadelphia on thirteen freight cars, the organ was too small to fill the cavernous spaces provided for her. Not a problem for Rodman: "As long as I live," he boasted, "we will continue to enlarge it until it combines the grandeur of a great organ with the tone colors and beauty of a great symphony orchestra."

One hundred years later, she is over twice as large as the original St. Louis organ. According to Peter Conte, "it's the size of three symphony orchestras."

Those unfamiliar with organs will appreciate its grandeur by comparing it with other organs. The world renowned Cavaillé-Col organ in Notre Dame Cathedral has 7,800 pipes. The Sydney Opera House grand organ boasts of 10,000. The Wanamaker has no fewer than 28,482—and the variety is equally staggering: Some pipes are as small as a child's pinky while the largest one, being 32 feet long, would allow the same child to play hide and seek inside.

The Curator

Back in the twenties, there were forty full-time employees looking after her. Today there are only two. One of them is Curt Mangel. He is the curator. However, this title in no way describes all he has done for an instrument described as "unplayable" in 1991 by Peter Conte. He has brought it back to life and describes what he does as a "labor of love." Now it is operating at 96 percent of its capacity.

Mr. Mangel has been interested in organs since he was a young boy and laments the fact he first visited the Grand Court only in the year 2000. Amazed by the organ's beauty, he also noticed it needed a lot of work. Realizing the importance of this instrument, he organized a group of professional volunteers to come in for one solid week to work on it. He ended up staying as a volunteer for five years. Lord and Taylor eventually hired him as a consultant.

I was able to go behind the scenes where the menagerie of pipes is located and saw firsthand the almost countless screws and bolts that were replaced to make it what it is today. I was in awe at the laborious precision of the restoration accomplished under the direction of this one man.

He is someone you cannot help but like, although he is a man of few words. When speaking about his work on this organ, he looks to the horizon as if to distance himself from the value of his labors, not wanting credit for the good he does.

The Friend

Wallace J. McLean is a proud volunteer with an organization called The Friends of the Wanamaker Organ. He is a 78-year-old man with the eyes of a 14-year-old. That was his age when he first heard the Wanamaker played. "I never forgot it," he said.

He derives an obvious joy being there and described his reason for becoming a volunteer very succinctly. "I have been taking from the organ all my life," he said. "It's payback time now." He speaks with passion about the organ as tears well up in his eyes.

Such enthusiasm is not uncommon around the Wanamaker. A shopper named Ethel May McSparren stopped by to give her testimony while we were speaking. She is from Lancaster, Penn., and first heard the organ around Christmastime when she was three years old. "I almost cried when I heard it start," she said. "I did not know they were still playing it. I wish my father were alive so he could hear this."

A Relic of the Past is Saved from the "God of Consumerism"

Before leaving, I saw a couple who seemed noticeably more moved than the rest. They were Mr. and Mrs. Robert Hoppe from Waverly, New York. They both looked well, considering they had just finished a six-hour train ride. Like the Frenchman, he too, was celebrating a birthday with a trip to see the Wanamaker, compliments of his wife.

"I could not have given him a better gift," said Mrs. Hoppe. "He was so happy when I told him we were coming, he was grinning from ear to ear." With camera in hand, she was snapping photos of the majestic organ pipes high above her while her husband stood in silent admiration.

He had acquired a taste for music some years ago, but admitted there was nothing like live music. Holding his hands up in an almost prayer-like gesture, he added, "But to think that Bose is coming close to reproducing this."

This comment said it all. Organs may come and go, but there is nothing like the Wanamaker anywhere else on planet earth. More impressive than its size and the appreciation of those who come from far and wide to hear it is the resolution of those determined to preserve her.

Many people would not expect to see Americans make the Herculean effort of these men to save such a relic of the past. Nor would they think it possible that a high-end store like Lord and Taylor would support this endeavor. I could almost hear them suggest piping computer-generated music behind the façade of this magnificent organ as an alternative to expensive repairs. Others might go a step further and suggest getting rid of the organ altogether. Sacrificing her to the "god of consumerism" would, after all, free up a lot of space which could be used for more merchandise.

However, that is not what Lord and Taylor chose to do. With the help of a dedicated curator, an accomplished organist, and a lot of dedicated friends, its sound is live and its appearance grand. It can be heard and appreciated—only in America.

CHAPTER 41

Virgin: It's Not a Dirty Word

BY NORMAN FULKERSON

When men dream, they accomplish things that appear to be impossible. They embrace ideals that seem to be impracticable. When aided by grace, we can move toward the good, true, and beautiful with supernatural strength and resolve. Thus, many of the things deemed too difficult by our secular society become part of the culture that elevates all. One of these is the virtue of purity. When strengthened by grace, virginity is possible and desirable.

Millions of teenagers nationwide, including male university students, have chosen to remain virgins until marriage. In doing so, they unflinchingly clash head on with a modern-day culture that implicitly condones free love.

A friend of mine was once riding the subway late at night when the doors opened and in stepped two couples returning from a night out on the town. They laughed and carried on until one of the ladies noticed a poster promoting abstinence on the wall behind them. She read it out loud to the others: "Virgin: It's not a dirty word." Then, half-jokingly, but with a voice that portrayed guilt and disappointment, she added, "Why didn't they tell us that when we were fifteen?" The nervous laughter that followed this remark quickly degenerated into a pensive silence and a marked note of frustration.

This young lady had obviously gone down a wrong path in life and briefly lamented not having been offered a different option.

It would appear that America is the last place on earth where a person who wants to maintain his virginity would find other options. Hollywood hardly misses an opportunity to glamorize impure lifestyles which corrupt our young people at home and project an incomplete image of America abroad. Freedom is supposed to be our motto, in all things, including love.

There is, however, a whole subculture in America that openly rejects impure lifestyles and immodest fashions. Members of this subculture fight to safeguard virginity and reject what they see as destructive trends and fashions. Young people across America are promising to remain pure until marriage and, by doing so, are proclaiming loudly and clearly that "virginity" as the sign said, "is not a dirty word." It is yet another "only in America" paradox.

* * *

Abstinence programs are a huge element in this trend. Over a billion dollars was given by the federal government in the early part of this century to programs that taught young people the value of remaining chaste until marriage. Millions more were allocated to bring this message to our Nation's classrooms. These programs focused not on the supposed benefits of condoms, but only how they fail. The fact that such programs existed reflects the fact that a certain sector of the American public wants to preserve virginity and make their voices heard. There are many abstinence groups nationwide, some of which promote seminars that culminate in purity pledges by teens.[1]

The Silver Ring Thing

The first time I began to take notice of such programs was when I saw a news item about a 15-year-old girl named Lydia Playfoot in West Sussex, England. She received international attention when authorities at the Millais All-Girls School told her to remove her purity ring. They said it was a transgression of the school's uniform policy. Her parents were upset because of the double standard this represented; practicing Muslims wearing headscarves and Sikhs using Kara bracelets in the same school went unmolested.[2]

The mention of an English girl in an article dealing with an American phenomenon might seem out of place. It is not. Lydia received her ring during a program presented by an American group called The Silver Ring Thing founded in 1996 by Denny Pattyn of Yuma, Arizona. His educational program aims at showing young people the physical, emotional, and spiritual problems resulting from an impure

---

1. "Taking the Pledge: *CBS News* Ed Bradley Reports on abstinence-only programs for reens," 60 Minutes, CBS, Sept. 18, 2005, http://www.cbsnews.com/stories/2005/ 05/20/60minutes/main696975.shtml.

2. Sarah Harris, "Wearing 'Purity Rings' Is banned at Girls' School," *Daily Mail*, Jun. 19, 2006.

lifestyle. "The only way to reverse the moral decay of any youth culture" he points out, "is to inspire a change in the conduct and behavior from those within the culture."[3]

Mr. Pattyn's group was formed in the shadow of another organization called True Love Waits, founded by Jimmy Hester in the early nineties. "We began to hear from students," Mr. Hester said, "that they did not have a way to express themselves about abstinence until marriage." In other words, they wanted to avoid taking a wrong path but did not see another option. "True Love Waits," he said, "grew out of that desire."

The commitment to remain pure initially entailed signing a pledge card which students carried in their pockets. Later on, the pledge card was replaced by a more visible and powerfully symbolic purity ring— a constant reminder of the promise made.

Purity rings are sometimes given by the father to the daughter, who will then give it to her future husband should she decide to marry. We can fully appreciate the beauty of this gesture when we consider the symbolism of brides wearing white to the altar. Queen Victoria was the first woman in the modern era to do so, but brides across Europe and America quickly followed the royal lead. The color white, formally symbolic of royal mourning, thus became more commonly the symbol of purity of heart, the innocence of childhood, and, later, virginity.[4]

Seeing so many young people wear such a visible sign of their chastity shatters the modern-day myth that no one is interested in remaining pure. Mr. Hester told an amusing story of one high school girl who evidently believed this myth. After taking the pledge, she stood up in her classroom and courageously affirmed, even if inaccurately, that she was the only virgin in the school. She was pleasantly surprised when several others corrected her: "You are not the only one, I am also." Millions of young people have taken the same pledge over the years.

True Manliness

It might appear from what has been said so far that those interested in such a concept are exclusively women. Virginity, after all, has more commonly been associated with women, while true manhood has

---

3. http://www.silverringthing.com

4. Blue was formally more common than white because of its association with the Virgin Mary.

been distorted by false archetypes. Men with piety are often presented as genderless beings that a young man would never want to imitate. On the opposite side of the spectrum is the equally distorted concept of men who are macho. Such men see the loss of virginity as not only an acceptable but even a necessary step towards their deformed image of manhood.

Sherif Girgis would be the first to disagree with these equally false options. "I personally found this intense struggle [to remain pure]," he said, "and the subsequent tranquility in having conquered self, to be eminently masculine."

Sherif Girgis, a co-founder of the Anscombe Society at Princeton.

He was a philosophy major at Princeton University where he co-founded the Anscombe Society which, among other things, promotes abstinence. The society is named after Elizabeth Anscombe, a Cambridge philosopher and staunch Roman Catholic who defended the Church's unpopular teaching on sexual ethics. A high point in her struggle came in 1968 when the Church reaffirmed its condemnation of contraception. While the intellectuals around her reacted with shock and rage, the Anscombe family toasted the decision with champagne.[5]

The society named in her honor has had similar struggles. Not long after they were formed, a particular group of people on campus, evidently not so enthusiastic about chastity, labeled them as homophobes. They might just have easily toasted with champagne. This did not deter them, and it was not long before they had an email list with 150 names.

According to Sherif, a convert to Catholicism like Mrs. Anscombe, the Princeton group has a twofold purpose. It not only provides a social network for like-minded people, but also provides intellectual arguments to help students grasp the importance of chastity in human development.

The most important thing, however, is to present a powerful example,

---

5. Robert P. George, "Elizabeth Anscombe, R.I.P.: One of the 20th century's most remarkable women," http://www.nationalreview.com/weekend/philosophy/philosophy-george020301.shtml.

especially for young men who lack proper role models. Cassandra Debenedetto is the other co-founder of Anscombe and the oldest of four siblings from Stow, Massachusetts. Her younger brothers appreciate the example given by students at Princeton. "Two of them plan to form an abstinence group at their high school," she said, "while the other hopes to do the same at the university he attends."

With the media coverage that followed their founding, the Anscombe Society was contacted by a similar group at Cornell University, said Cody May. He was a 19-year-old philosophy major from Center, Texas, and former officer of Anscombe. "Although [the Cornell group] did not get the same publicity we did," he explained, "they just wanted to say 'Hey, we are with you and we are offering similar things here at Cornell.'"[6]

Jonathan Butler, a 19-year-old Catholic student at the University of Colorado at Boulder was with them as well. Known to many as the "People's Republic of Boulder," the University of Colorado is the last place on earth you would expect to find "right-wing fanatics" promoting chastity—especially if they are male. That didn't stop Jonathan and his three friends from founding the College Coalition for Relationship Education. Such an innocuous title is understandable when you consider the ire liberals have for such groups promoting chastity.

There were similar clubs at the University of Northern Colorado and Colorado State University. Jonathan hopes to have help, after he graduates, from fellow students in taking this message to the younger crowds. "I would like to see members of my college," he said, "visiting grade schools to teach them [about the abstinence message] also."

Modesty as a Safeguard of Virginity

The subject of modesty unexpectedly came up while I was speaking with Cody May. Coming from a very hot Center, Texas, he commented on the "unexpected blessing" of going to Princeton, with temperatures that oblige girls to dress decently. Cody is not the only one who thinks that way at Princeton. "More men than women would agree with me," he said. "Men recognize the problem because if affects them so badly." He understood that to maintain virginity without the virtue of modesty

---

6. A Cornell Law School professor condemned such programs because he said they endorse a religious agenda. http://www.news.cornell.edu/releases/Nov00/Simson.sex.ed.html.

is hard, if not impossible.

Cassandra Debenedetto would agree with him wholeheartedly. Besides being one of the founders of the Anscombe Society, she also used to have her own blog appropriately titled, "Modestly Yours." In one of her entries, she tells of her experience of training high school girls and how impressed she was with their grasp of modesty. "The girls understood that modest dress did not mean wearing baggy or "frumpy" clothing. . . . Rather, they understood that one can dress fashionably and in a way that accents her femininity without dressing in a revealing or distracting way."[7]

This idea may be catching on. Teenage girls in Tucson, Arizona, got so fed up with the indecent clothing which they were being offered at stores that they circulated a petition demanding more modest fashions. Over 4,000 students signed a petition that got the attention of Dillard's, which ended up holding a fashion show to spotlight more modest attire.[8]

Then there is the case of Mrs. Rita Davidson, who drove five hours from Ontario, Canada, across the American border precisely because of the modesty issue. "I wanted to meet my pen pal from California who once commented that she always wears a dress."

"This stance intrigued me," she said, "since it seemed so severe." Upon meeting her American pen pal, she was attracted by her very feminine manners and sincerity. "Her whole image struck me," she continued, "and a seed was planted." That seed later developed into a lay organization called Martyrs of Purity, which is a crusade to save souls, not only from impurity, but immodesty as well. She was quickly forced to open a post office box in New York. "Ninety percent of our customers are American," she said. "Catholic families in America take their faith more seriously."

* * *

There are those who will read this article and quickly question the longevity of the purity pledges made by millions of young people. Liberals will do so—backed by statistics—because they want to continue

---

7. "A Hopeful Generation," Modestly Yours, June 28, 2006, http://blogs.modestlyyours.net/modestly_yours/2006/06/a_ hopeful_gener.html.

8. Scott Simonson, "Local Teens Score One for Modesty," *Arizona Daily Star,* Sept.18, 2004.

handing out contraception. Others will do so for a different reason. They will argue that the young people who take these pledges are doomed to fail because they have voluntarily immersed themselves in a promiscuous culture. They will also question the integrity of university students who courageously defend their virginity on liberal campuses, even if it is sprinkled with a modesty message.

This article was not intended to portray America as a convent, which it most certainly is not. It was to point out the paradoxical desire to remain virginally pure on the part of young people in a country and culture that, at least implicitly, condones free love.

This is the paradox which was so well expressed by that poor soul on the subway: "Why didn't they tell us that when we were fifteen?" She had experienced the empty pleasures the world offers and was candid enough to raise a very prickly question: "Why wasn't I offered another option?"

Hidden inside this question is a desire for something else and an affirmation that, if offered another option, "I might have taken it!" Was this subway lady aware of the millions whose desire for virginity led them to make pledges to remain pure? Did she know that those same people unashamedly wear purity rings as an outward sign of that promise and often face ridicule for doing so? Did she know about female students, not much older than she, at an Ivy League school that are proudly promoting modesty? What about the men attending the same school who appreciated these efforts? Or what about these same men who choose virginity, and in doing so, smash the false archetypes of wimpy or macho men in the process?

She, like you, might have been unaware that such a paradox not only exists, but is alive and well—*only in America.*

CHAPTER 42

Trooping the Colors at Brown University

BY JOHN HORVAT II

When men dream, it often comes about in a very organic, unplanned way. It may start with a decision to pursue some artistic desire or hobby. The dream then expands to become more than a passing fancy but rather a marvelous avocation that pays tribute to the great feats of men. Such is the case of an extraordinary lady who put together an amazing collection of toy soldiers now housed at one of America's oldest universities.

There is something about toy soldiers that brings out the boy in every man.

Before toys became genderless and pacifistic, the toy soldier was the mainstay of countless boyhood games. How many boys marched their soldiers into battle, staged mock wars, and dreamed of military glory! Indeed, how many military careers were born on the humble battlegrounds of living room floors?

My thoughts were far from such childhood musings when I approached Brown University's library in Providence, Rhode Island. At the entrance, I chanced to see a sign mentioning the Anne S.K. Brown Military Collection on the fifth floor.

Brown University houses a huge toy soldier collection.

Intrigued, I walked up the flights of stairs and down the hallway. Upon reaching the door, I rang the bell. The librarian, a military researcher, craned his neck out, asked what I wanted, and then let me in.

Never in my wildest dreams did I imagine what I would find. I had stumbled upon America's foremost documentary resource of soldiers and soldiering, one of the world's largest collections devoted to the study of military uniforms—and a wonderland of toy soldiers.

How did such a military collection end up on a liberal American campus? Only in America can you find such a paradox.

A Wonderland of Soldiers

There they were: toy soldiers, thousands of them, all in brilliant, colorful uniforms. In lighted vitrines, display after display of military toy soldiers in battle array represented fighting men and their units from the days of ancient Egypt to the twentieth century.

There were Egyptian chariots, Roman legions, and Persian armies. There were exquisitely detailed medieval knights on horseback and displays of Renaissance armor. There were Gordon Highlanders, Irish Guards, the Black Watch, and the most celebrated regiments of Britain and France. I marveled at glamorous nineteenth-century uniforms of every nationality with all their splendor and display.

I also found familiar historic figures. There were Charlemagne, Saint Joan of Arc, and famous crusaders. I saw others ranging from Louis XIV to Robert E. Lee to Churchill. It was a veritable procession of history.

It did not stop there. Amid the 288 feet of displayed soldiers, I found turbaned Indian troops on elephants, robed Bedouins on camels, bandoliered Boers, and rampaging Zulus.

Finally, there was a host of displays of military and royal pomp and

Display after display of toy soldiers make up the Anne S.K. Brown Military Collection.

circumstance. Not least among these was a spectacular English coronation with all its splendor. Above all, I could not contain my enthusiasm for the scene of a papal parade, featuring the Vicar of Christ in a gilded carriage surrounded by Swiss and Noble Guards.

I was spellbound. Like a young boy reliving battles past, I spent the next two hours in awed wonder.

A Vast Collection

The next day I returned to find out more about this extraordinary collection. Library curator Peter Harrington was only too happy to answer my questions.

I learned that the collection contains more than just toy soldiers. Presently, there are over 12,000 printed books, 18,000 albums, sketchbooks, scrapbooks, and portfolios, and over 13,000 individual works of art dedicated to military themes.

To my surprise, I also learned that the library was the life-work of one person—and that person was an extraordinary lady.

The Extraordinary Mrs. Brown

Anne Seddon Kinsolving was born on March 25, 1906, in Brooklyn, New York. Her parents were both members of the Virginia aristocracy with impressive lineages. Her father eventually became rector of Old St. Paul's Episcopal Church in downtown Baltimore where she spent her childhood.

Anne S. K. Brown, the extraordinary lady who put the collection together.

From her earliest days, Anne developed a penchant for all things military. She traced this love to a treasured copy of *The Wonder Book of Soldiers for Boys and Girls* given to her on her ninth birthday. She was also impressed by the parades and uniforms she saw in Baltimore during World War I.

In 1930, she married John Nicholas Brown, heir to one of the oldest fortunes in America. During their honeymoon in Europe, the new bride decided to buy a "few" toy soldiers to decorate a room in their home in Providence. Those few soldiers became a veritable army.

Beginning of a Collection

Mrs. Brown was not the type of person who was content to own these soldiers; she wanted to identify and know them. She embarked on a quest to catalog her troops, concentrating on those from the seventeenth century onward. With great energy, she contacted booksellers on military costumes in Boston, New York, Philadelphia, and other major cities, and she made numerous sorties into the backrooms of those shops in search of prints, drawings, and illustrated books. She also wrote books on military subjects and became a leading authority on military collections and uniforms.

A papal parade, featuring the Vicar of Christ in a gilded carriage surrounded by Swiss and Noble Guards.

Not satisfied with the domestic market, Mrs. Brown made forays overseas and soon began acquiring books and prints from all over Europe. When World War II broke out, a bomb fell on Ackermann's, a major military publisher in London. That incident spurred her into launching an extensive importing operation, giving her agents carte blanche to buy any military art to save it from the ravages of war.

The postwar years saw her broadening her collection with further acquisitions. According to Mr. Harrington, however, she made little effort to collect modern khaki uniforms because their egalitarian design was drab and "there was little difference between the soldiers' and officers' uniforms."

Wanting to organize her collection better, she eventually hired a full-time librarian, who arranged it in its present form. The collection outgrew the Browns' home and, by the time of her death in 1985, the whole collection had been gradually transferred to Brown University Library, where it remains as a legacy to her passion.

An Attraction to Heroism

The fascinating story of Mrs. Brown is but part of the story of her toy soldiers. I asked Mr. Harrington what had attracted her to them, and he responded that it was something more than just an eccentric fancy.

Mrs. Brown had noted that the picturesque beauty of the uniforms themselves is not what leads men to honor the soldier. Actors and acrobats, she observed, can be equally charming. No, what attracts us is a higher ideal symbolized in these men in uniform. There one sees expressed the moral beauty inherent in military life: the elevation of sentiments, and the willingness to shed one's blood for a higher cause. One sees the strength for undertaking, for suffering, risking, and winning.

The beauty of the military uniform speaks of the moral nobility of a fight that is entirely based upon ideas of honor, and of force placed at the service of good and turned against evil. It is the joy of serving with courage, strength, discipline, and heroism that allows the soldier to live in an atmosphere of legend and glory. It is only right that the uniform express these values with color, pomp, and ceremony that attract the multitudes.

Alas, such sentiments find little sympathy in the postmodern man who puts no ideal above self. Today's pacifists hold an erroneous idea of peace whereby conflict must be avoided at all cost, even at the sacrifice of principles. This is not true peace, but the stagnant "peace" of moral decay.

True peace, as Saint Augustine teaches, is the tranquility of order— above all, Christian order. In this, peace is a fruit of an order that must sometimes be defended. Soldiers have sacrificed themselves from time immemorial so that people can have this true peace.

That is why their legends live on—even in the toy soldiers who depict their deeds.

When asked during a speech she gave in 1961 why so many people have portrayed the soldier, Mrs. Brown quite aptly replied, "I prefer to believe it was because, as men, they were admired and respected, even when they were feared, and that over the years the men who themselves had no urge to pioneer and endure the heat of battle, the artists and poets and composers, felt in their hearts a debt of gratitude to the military men who have earned them the privilege of living in peace. So they made these men immortal."

CHAPTER 43

The Third Place

BY NORMAN FULKERSON

When men dream, they often need a place to bond and collect themselves. It is those informal gathering places like smoke rooms that provide a way for many Americans to transcend their hectic daily lives and "solve the world's problems." The formula of a proper place and a group of people who feel comfortable there sets the stage for dreams to happen. All need to have their own places to philosophize and idealize their lives together in society.

Years ago, I had the chance to visit Italy. I loved my stay there and had an amusing experience in the airport the day of my departure. While standing in line to check my bags, an employee announced that our flight would be delayed. The next man in line went ballistic and vented his anger on the lady who was checking us in. "This is terrible," he said. "I'll miss my appointment." He went into great detail about how all of this was really of earth-shattering importance.

The Italian lady stood calmly and listened, with a sympathetic look and a pensive gaze. She could just as easily have been watching a popular Italian opera as listening to an American complaining about the tragedy of a delayed flight. He eventually finished his operatic dramatization of the disaster of his altered travel plans. She looked at him with her droopy eyes and serene face, and all she had to say was, "Compared to life, it's not that bad."

This was a memorable experience for me since it gave me a brief glimpse of two opposing philosophies! On one side of the counter was the stereotypical "time is money" philosophy, which cannot tolerate an unplanned moment, while on the other side was a "joy of life" philosophy that welcomes the spontaneous moments that enrich life.

Such situations are a chance to take a deserved break for some, but for our businessman, it was a source of anger and frustration. His world is one of travel planners and nifty computer programs to schedule his every minute. His life is a succession of airports, taxis, hotel rooms, business lunches, or quick burgers at McDonald's, then quickly off again to some other destination to close yet another deal.

Fortuitous circumstances that allow a moment of relaxation are con-

sidered vile intruders in his world of production. An outsider witnessing such a scene might think that America is simply one big machine,
with man playing the part of cogs in a massive industrial wheel.

Those who think this way have missed a growing trend.

With the cigar boom of the mid-nineties, smoke rooms for men
sprouted up in almost every major city in the country. Since my first
trip to Italy, I began to notice how these rooms are a haven for men
who long for more than time management.

Riding the crest of this new wave was Denver's elegant Brown Palace
Hotel. They simply took what was formerly a small bar servicing their
Atrium Lounge, added a wall in 1996, and transformed it into a cigar
bar named after Winston Churchill. In its first year of operation, "the
Churchill Bar did $1 million worth of business, a 500 percent increase
over the previous year. There are between 3,000 and 4,000 people on the
bar's mailing list, which continues to grow." What is the attraction? The
reason is simple: "Cigars force you to stop and do something that is
pleasurable for at least one part of your day," said one regular of the bar.[1]

"The Great Good Place"

Americans avidly search for such informal "third places" that will provide them with the elements necessary for a relaxing conversation.

Ray Oldenburg in his book *The Great Good Place* says that "Great
civilizations, like great cities, share a common feature. Evolving within
them and crucial to their growth and refinement are distinctive informal public gathering places." Most men need an occasional break from
work and home. What is often missing is that unique third place where
they can get together with other men to enjoy a simple yet satisfying
pleasure of life: conversation.[2]

Women may have their Victorian tearoom escapes to enjoy a nice
chat, but now many American men have also found an escape. This
provides us with the paradox that, in a nation that promoted the "time-
is-money philosophy," you also find a good number of men who appreciate fine tobacco and the relaxation their third place provides.

Such third places are common in Europe. It is difficult to imagine
an Irishman without a pub close by to enjoy a pint of Guinness and

---

1. Frank T Andorka, Jr., "Cigar Bars," *Hotel and Motel Management*, Vol. 212, no. 10 (Jun.
2, 1997), 50.

2. Ray Oldenburg, *The Great Good Place* (New York: 1989), xv.

discuss politics. French cafés supply the necessary ambiance for speaking openly about philosophical currents of the day, and the beer halls of Germany are the breeding ground for new ideas. Similar places also exist in America, however, and their role in society is becoming more important. Mr. Oldenburg's blueprint of the third place provides necessary elements to see that such locations provide the same benefits for Americans that Europeans enjoy in their pubs, coffee houses, and beer halls.

Almost every town in America has its local diner, which is not just a place to get an inexpensive breakfast and hot cup of coffee—good portions of conviviality are served up as well. The corner barbershop is a frequent stop for retired men who want someone to talk to, and the public squares of many cities provide more than a park bench in the shade to rest on a hot day.

The common denominator among all of these places is the note of surprise. Who will show up today? Those who do are always welcome, since frequenters of the third place are people with loads of personality and lots to say. So the ordinary stop at the barber, the diner, or the park bench becomes an experience that enriches life as few things can.

The Regular, the Newcomer, and the Bore

According to Oldenburg, there are many distinct characteristics that make up a third place. The third place is comfortable, a home away from home. It is a place that has its regulars, but also the occasional newcomer who adds a fresh element to the ambience. "What attracts the regular visitor to the third place," says Oldenburg, "are the fellow customers." Informal meeting places are "upbeat because those who enjoy them ration the time they spend there." Besides the "regulars" and the "newcomers," he also describes another type: the bore. He is the one who has "long since lost that edge that makes people interesting, an edge that is honed by confrontation with life outside." While the regular and the newcomer leave "before the magic fades," the bore has a tendency to hang on forever, milking the moment for all its worth.

The reason informal meeting places are upbeat is simple: It is a place where the pretensions of work and the responsibilities of home can be put aside. It provides us with the situation and surroundings in which we can be ourselves and explore our ideas and dreams in a neutral environment with non-threatening participants.

Smoke-rooms are perhaps the best examples of the "third place" for men that I found. Born over 300 years ago in London, the gentleman's club or smoke room was an essential element in the social life of men, described by one astute observer as "mausoleums of masculine inactivity."[3]

"Where the Problems of the World Are Solved"

It was an overcast day as I walked down the cobblestone walkway of what I later learned is the gentleman's quarter or arcade. It is the oldest part of Nashville, a place where men of the past gathered to do business. This area of town was home to the Arcade Smoke Shop, where men of the present remembered the past. The closely laid cobblestones seemed analogous to the close friendships that were formed, strengthened, and solidified in the Arcade. Housed in the oldest building in town, it was a popular gathering place for Nashville men.

My visit to the Arcade proved to be an experience. Tennesseans by nature are a very hospitable people, and as I entered the shop, I immediately felt at home due to the kind treatment of the owner, Wilson Frazier.

"Do you get a lot of customers here," I asked. "Yes, sir," he said, pointing to a couch pushed up against the wall, "the problems of the world are solved right there." With such a small sitting area, I figured there couldn't be more than a handful at any given time. When I returned during lunchtime to see who it was that solved the world's problems, I found a constant flow of men coming and going.

The Arcade Smoke Shop was the classic example of a third place, as defined by Oldenburg, "where individuals may come and go as they please and in which none are required to play host and in which all feel at home and comfortable."

Patrick Owen was a regular of the Arcade and is the owner of his own smoke room up the street. He works for the Department of Human Services in downtown Nashville and does Civil War reenacting as a hobby.

"Why do men come to these smoke rooms?" I asked him.

"Men need the company of other men," he said, "time to recapture camaraderie. Smoke rooms give them the opportunity to discuss tra-

---

3. Jolee Edmondson, "Clubland," *Cigar Aficionado*, Mar./Apr. 1997.

ditional things." Men need a place to relax with other men and pound out those perplexing questions that have been ruminating in their head during the day. The segregation of sexes "accounts for the origins of the third place," says Oldenburg, "and remains the basis for much of the appeal and benefits this institution has to offer." Men sometimes need to be with other men, as ladies often need to be with other ladies.

Patrick is an archetypal example of a Civil War re-enactor. When he first greets you, there is the characteristic bow of the head, and the gentlemanly usage of the title "sir." He doesn't just barge into a conversation, but is the champion of a smooth entrance and gentle transition. His mannerisms were thus more civilized, like someone of the nineteenth century. He was polite, chivalrous, a joy to be around. "The smoke rooms of today are like the campfires during the time of the Civil War, where men would gather to converse," he said.

"We have always needed this type of thing," he continued. "The Greeks had their agora—an ancient marketplace of Greece; the Romans had the Forum—the public square where laws were read; early Americans had taverns and coffee houses."

Suddenly I found myself engaged in an elevated conversation surrounded by a pensive group of men, some puffing on cigars, others drawing from elegantly shaped pipes. Waiting my turn to speak I was amused by the sign hanging on the wall overhead: "A pipe gives a wise man time to think, and a fool something to put in his mouth."

"Do Angels Have Free Will?"

This experience in conversational cuisine is by no means restricted to Nashville's Arcade. While visiting Rae's Tobacco Shop in Harrisburg, Pennsylvania, one day, I unexpectedly found myself drawn into a theological debate with one of the regulars, David Ravegum, on the existence of angels and whether or not they have free wills. With the help of a friend, I was able to explain that they do. Upon leaving, David looked at me and said, "You have piqued my interest. I am going to go home and read up on the angels." The next time I visited Rae's, David recognized me and affirmed, "You are right, angels do have free will."

The men who frequent the Tobacco Chandler in Hanover, Pennsylvania, enjoy conversations more along the sociological line: "What is happening with the youth of today? Why don't they have respect for elders?" One such conversation was so interesting that Mike Evans,

the owner, suggested that we invite some of the area youth to participate. Instead of just playing billiards on Mike's table, he felt they could
also benefit from the simple pleasure of an elevated conversation.

The Humidour in Cockeysville, Maryland, provides a dignified ambience for its customers, with leather armchairs, rich wood paneling,
a splendid air freshener, and large crystal ashtrays. Don Curtis of the
National Investors Company is one of the regulars. Don is a master
conversationalist with whom it is easy to talk and who has a lot to say.
His concerns are more of a political nature and, when I first met him,
he wasted no time in venting his anger over the myriad scandals surrounding the Clinton administration, especially the moral ones. "If we
are not careful," he said, "we could end up like the Roman Empire, rot-
ting from within. If that happens, we won't need an outside invader,
we will simply give up."

Back in Nashville. . .

Before leaving the Arcade, Wilson Frazier was kind enough to show
me the upstairs of the shop. As we reached the top of the stairs, a dimly
lit sitting area caught my eye. Two comfortable armchairs faced each
other with a table between them. Arranged on the table was a chess-
board ready for play. Outside the window was a bird's-eye view of the
cobblestone arcade below. The back room had a conference table
where some men go to escape the agitation of the workplace. "It gives
them the opportunity," Mr. Frazier said, "to get away from their offices,
secretaries, and noisy phones."

The smoke rooms of America are a strong indicator that some men
are becoming increasingly dissatisfied with the rat race and desire a
solution to the rush of everyday life. The cigar boom provided the ex-
cuse, the smoke room the place—a third place "where the problems
of the world are solved."

CHAPTER 44

Tea, Anyone?

BY NORMAN FULKERSON

When we dream, we construct special ambiences to which we can retreat and think about the important things of life. The tearoom is one of these third places that provide a portal to an ideal world that speaks to the soul of elegance, manners, and tradition. These places provide occasions for leisure and conversation, so needed in a world of frenetic intemperance.

What impressed me were the details, those little touches that created an ambience and put me at ease. Here was a calm spot away from the crowded fast-food places, where one is not an anonymous person dashing down a meal.

"Take your time," my waitress said as she removed my plate, leaving just the elegant teacup in place. I calmly finished sipping my tea and continued pondering the scene around me. No, it wasn't England or even close to it, I'll grant you, but it did take a little adjusting to realize that here I was, having afternoon tea in a tearoom—in rural Pennsylvania.

The place was called The Black Rose of Hanover, not without a little touch of Victorian splendor. I must admit that the sight of it piqued my interest as I passed through the semi-industrial town of Hanover. It was a pleasant surprise—an oasis amid the noisy and frantic rhythm of daily life.

I was even more surprised to hear that I would not be alone in enjoying my afternoon tea. Tearooms like The Black Rose are becoming very popular all across the United States. Hundreds are sprouting up in the most unlikely places.

Tearooms in the land of fast food! Such an incongruity! "Only in America," I thought.

It is not as if tea is not popular here. After all, aside from plain water, tea is the most widely consumed beverage in the world and is found in almost 80 percent of American households. According to the Tea Council of

© Pamela Mcadams | Dreamstime.com

the U.S.A., on any given day, nearly 127 million Americans drink tea. In these tranquil tearoom retreats, however, one finds much more than just a beverage competing with water. One finds a way of life.

I decided to investigate The Black Rose to see if I could find out more. When I called to arrange for tea, I was told that the waiting list for Saturday tea is four weeks. A quick sigh of relief was my response since I was considering a weekday. "It would still be good to call a day ahead to make sure there is an opening," was the friendly response on the other end of the line.

In our industrialized world, accustomed to eating on the run, where time is money, it would appear that people want a little more out of life. That is exactly what owner Helen Widdowson seeks to give them with her establishment.

Having spent eight years in Germany, she is impressed by the difference of life in Europe. She liked those "third" kind of places outside the home and the workplace where people can get together for leisurely conversation. Apparently, she wasn't the only one looking for such retreats. After just eighteen months of operation, she is already considering expanding her tearoom, and with good reason, for business is booming.

Who goes to the tearoom? Nearly everyone, it seems. Mrs. Widdowson's clients are not mere eccentric Anglophiles, but pretty much a cross section of the local population: businessmen, housewives, even teenagers. It is a trend mirrored in other tearooms across the country.

"Why do they come and what motivated you to open a tearoom?" I asked Mrs. Widdowson.

"Our country is uncivil today. People don't talk because we live in a fast-paced world where everything is packaged and instant. People are searching for civility in their lives," she replied.

Indeed, there is something about the atmosphere that imparts that exact impression. Observing a couple of ladies nearby, I sensed a refreshing cordiality.

"They're under a lot of stress," she continued, "working too many hours. A tea break works because it's deliberate. It causes you to slow down and focus on some other person or yourself. The experience of tea is about relationships."

Yes, whom will I take next time I go?

In nearby Gettysburg, the Thistlefields English Tearoom goes even further. Authenticity reaches the point that you will occasionally see modern Victorians wearing period clothing, complete with hats and gloves. Afternoon tea there is a serious affair.

Amateur theatrics, one might think, yet it appears to be something more. Tea speaks to the soul. It calls to mind principles that seem so distant.

The Bigham House Bed and Breakfast in Holmes, Ohio, for example, invites prospective guests to "an authentic English Tea Room in Grand Victorian Style" where they can "step back in time to a bygone era of Victorian elegance and charm."

At the Devon Tea Room in the quaint Cape Cod village of West Dennis, Massachusetts, a similar spirit reigns. "It is exciting . . . to see that all over America, people are discovering or rediscovering the pleasures of tea," claims the tearoom's promotional literature. "For many, a traditional afternoon tea party brings back wonderful memories."

At the very aptly named Magnolia and Ivy Tearoom in the "good ole South" in Plains, Georgia, Terri Eager not only manages the shop, but also teaches others all over the country how to open their own tearooms. She says that people, including teenagers, visit her three shops because "they don't feel comfortable with the cyber-future." She not only serves tea but, for those who feel they need a bit of polishing, she offers a variety of etiquette classes: "Tea Etiquette," "Children's Etiquette and Dining," and "Corporate Etiquette," trained and certified by the Protocol School of Washington.

Perhaps that is the whole secret of the tearoom. Amid the triumphant vulgarity of an increasingly egalitarian world and the noisy, frantic, and hurly-burly pace of daily life, tradition appears as an elevated rest for the soul. It represents good sense, good breeding, good order, and the art of living wisely.

For this reason, even a distant tradition from England can find sympathy. It explains why some Americans have a penchant for all things English. Despite its censurable romantic aspects, the Victorian archetype has its restful attractions that temper our fast-paced modernity. We long for the thatched cottages, the English gardens, and the picturesque hamlets popularized by American artist Thomas Kinkaid. Such topics are typically found in Victorian-themed magazines, which treat readers to features from this not-so-bygone era.

Above all, such trends serve to stress how people need tradition—

especially our Christian tradition. Tradition is not just the past, but an indispensable element that must rule the present. It keeps equality from sweeping away all refinement and enthroning vulgarity. It prevents freedom from serving as a pretext for chaos and depravity. Without tradition, the fast pace of technology enslaves man by turning him into a machine. Only tradition provides that mysterious something that makes life meaningful, human, and bearable.

While casually sipping my tea at The Black Rose, I could not help but feel that I had been denied something very special for too long. I was comforted by the realization that I was not alone. The story has it that a long time ago there was a young English girl who was also denied the special delight of having a leisurely cup of tea. When she grew up and made a name for herself in this world, when people recognized her as somebody, one of the first things she did—after her coronation as Queen Victoria of England—was order a cup of tea.

Tearooms have become very popular places of rest for the soul.

CHAPTER 45

Tallyho!

BY NORMAN FULKERSON

When men dream, they find ways of doing difficult tasks in an elegant and elevated fashion. They surround these undertakings with ceremony, symbols, and tradition, beauty and polish. Such is the case of foxhunting, which began as a means of pest control and evolved into a social event filled with pageantry and legend.

I t was a cool, crisp morning as I drove down a Pennsylvania back road on the way to my first fox hunt. The sky was clear and blue, and the bright sunshine illuminating the frost-covered field brought an agreeable white freshness to the landscape.

The sights along the way were what one would expect in rural America: small town gas stations, a local post office, and a sign for the local taxidermist. I knew I must be close to my destination, the Rose Tree Fox Hunting Club, the oldest such club in America, having been founded in 1859. There I met my host, Joseph Murtagh, the master of the hounds, known to the other fox hunters as Jody. His tie pin immediately caught my attention: Its golden fox matched the weathervane atop his barn.

My initial impression was that Jody is typically American, very candid, and straightforward. "You can ride along in the truck if you wish to follow the hunt," he said, "and anytime you care to leave, they would bring you back." After he had mounted his horse to leave, I noticed a subtle change: Joseph Murtagh became rather more distinguished, his deportment more elevated, his manners more refined.

What happened, I asked myself, *at that moment between the ground and the saddle?* He sat astride his shiny black thoroughbred like anyone about to go for a ride, but there was something different. Was it the scarlet jacket we Americans so often link to a

Joseph Murtagh, third from left.

foxhunt, or the snowy white breeches? It could have been his shiny black riding boots or the English hunting horn stuck into his polished brown saddle.

He seemed to me the epitome of an English gentleman as the excited hounds were released and bounded all around him. It was only as the group of hunters trotted off with the clip-clop of hoofs on the frozen ground, though, that I realized what had changed in Jody Murtagh. While in the saddle, he becomes part of a tradition that dates back centuries. More specifically, he is the bearer of that same tradition here in America, since he happens to be the fourth-generation master of the hounds for the oldest club in America.

Foxhunting has been around since time immemorial, but became popular in its present form in England as a means of culling the fox population. Farmers have a hard enough time making ends meet without foxes dining on their chickens and small lambs. What began as a practical solution to a real problem later developed into a tradition rich in ceremony and etiquette.

All of that is now being attacked in the U.K. by animal-rights groups and used as a lever for a political agenda. In 2004, the British Parliament voted to outlaw foxhunting in England and Wales, forcing the country most typically known for foxhunting to hang up the dignified attire and find other less elevated means of controlling its rust-colored pests.

Before anyone takes down those magnificent foxhunting prints, so often seen in American homes, for fear of suddenly being politically incorrect, hold on. There may be a war against foxhunting in Europe, but this aristocratic sport is still very much alive here in the United States.

Authentically British

Barbara Murtagh, Jody's wife, is a distinguished lady full of zest for life. A former fox hunter who has taken some spills, she has long since hung up her riding clothes, but she still relishes having breakfast ready for the hunters when they return. Her eyes sparkle with a childlike enthusiasm when she speaks about foxhunting. I had never encountered anything like it before and was perfectly content just listening.

We found ourselves on a hill, high above south central Pennsylvania when Barbara suddenly shouted with enthusiasm, "There he goes! Tallyho!" Running across the frost-covered cornfield was a red fox, with a tightly grouped pack of excited hounds, Jody, and the rest of the hunters in vigorous pursuit.

Scarlet and black jackets, white breeches, and polished black boots—what a sight! This is no ordinary hunt, I thought; this is civilized. It should be, since the fox chase in America meticulously models itself after its British counterpart, with the exception that the fox is not killed in America. Everything else, from the hierarchy of the hunt to the clothing, is authentic.

Hierarchy and Dress Code

As the master, Jody is in charge. After him are the whips or "whipper-ins," who control the hounds, knowing each dog by name and caring for them as one would a child. Yes, they carry a whip, but they do not use it on the animals; they only crack it to keep the hounds together. The master's responsibility, with the help of the whips, is simple: Find a fox. Once this is done, he blows his horn to notify the field master, who then invites the field to join the chase.

The blessing of the hounds is a part of the tradition surrounding fox hunting.

The field master's job is keeping the field of riders close enough to enjoy watching the hounds, yet not so close as to interfere with the master or huntsman in pursuit of his hounds. This strict hierarchy is also accompanied by a formal dress code. Every hunt has two seasons: cub hunting, when young hounds are introduced into the pack, and the formal season. The cubbing season, or "ratcatcher," allows for less formal attire.

Ratcatchers normally mean the use of a tweed jacket with a shirt and tie or turtleneck. November marks the beginning of the formal season and the donning of scarlet coats and white jodhpurs, or riding breeches. Wearing the pinks, as the coats are called, is a privilege one must earn. Others wear black coats. The collars of the coats are full of meaning as well, since different colors signify varying levels in the club hierarchy.

The formal season begins with the traditional Saint Hubert's day Mass and blessing of the hounds. Saint Hubert lived in the eighth century and was known for his love of hunting stags. One evening while hunting in the Ardennes of northern France, he encountered the largest deer he had ever seen. This deer was different, however. Between its antlers was a gold cross glowing with an unearthly light. Young Hubert took this as a sign that he was to enter the priesthood. He eventually became the patron saint of hounds and hunting, not only because he had been such a valiant huntsman, but because the hounds he bred are the foundation stock of nearly every hound in the world today.

What to Do with All These Foxes?

Those who think that this is a sport practiced by a few eccentric Americans grasping for some link with bygone days are mistaken. There are currently 177 recognized hunts across America, comprising some 20,000 mounted fox hunters. For the most part, they are governed by the Masters of Foxhounds Association of America (MFHA) located in Leesburg, Virginia.

Lt. Col. Dennis Foster, Ret., the executive director of the MFHA, is upset with the unreasonable demands made by the animal-rights activists in England—demands that ended a rich tradition. He has a right to be angry.

According to conservative estimates, there are over 450,000 foxes in England. In an article in the *Wall Street Journal-Europe*, Frederick Forsyth points out that foxes "breed about 1.5 times their number in cubs. They grow fast, too," he says. "Born in February, weaned in May, they are ready to hunt, kill, and breed in October. The staple diet is wild rabbit.... In frosty winters they will turn in hunger to poultry and newborn lambs." The necessity to cull the fox population is therefore indisputable.

The question, then, is, "How?" Of all the different methods available—traps, neck snares, gas, poison, shotguns, rifles—trained hounds have been the choice of country people. It is a good choice, for it is at once the most humane and the most dignified option.

However, foxhunting "has gone beyond a mere eco-necessity," Forsyth continued. "It has become a rural society event clothed in ritual and pageantry" which "drives the political left wing to transports of rage."

Symbols of Restraint

So this is not merely a dispute over the well-being of a poor little fox, but rather a profound sociological difference of opinion. There are those who have a problem with ceremony and manners that elevate and refine. They forget God's command in Genesis that men rule over every creature that moves upon the earth. It is thus that the refined individual who enjoys the fox chase becomes a symbol of restraint, good manners, and elevation in contrast to those who prefer an untamed and wild nature, symbolic of bad passions left ungoverned.

Moreover, animal rights activists hardly practice what they preach. The acts of violence in England against fox hunters, such as letter bombs and attacks on innocent humans by club-wielding fanatics lead one to believe that we may soon need an organization to protect men rather than foxes.

What is necessary, however, is an appreciation for the good manners, decency, and proper deportment displayed by fox hunting enthusiasts all across America.

Nancy Hannum understands this all very well. She is the master of the hounds in Chester County, Pennsylvania, and is considered by other hunt fans as "a member of the old hierarchy." This elderly matron has been hunting since she was four. "She is the only lady I know," said Barbara Murtagh, "who can command without losing her femininity." Mrs. Hannum told me that "Fox hunting is a family affair, and that is the reason I like it. When the children were young, I would walk down to the barn like a *grand dame* with my husband, since they had our horses saddled and ready to go." Foxhunting teaches discipline and ceremony, which shows in the field during a hunt. She also spoke of a young man who had been working for them just a short while: "The change that occurred in him was remarkable," she said. "He became a gentleman. If you come for a visit," she continued, "you are treated with respect and the title of 'Mister'." This comes from the "association with people who do things right."

One lady I spoke with said she happened upon a foxhunt while driving home from work one day. "I couldn't believe my eyes," she said. "We quickly got our camera out and took pictures. It was so beautiful."

We cannot deny, then, that the center of the debate over foxhunting is not the killing or mistreating of animals, but an erroneous philosophy and egalitarian vision of the universe which places animals not just on equal footing with, but superior, to men. In this worldview, an innocent human life is fair game, as seen in abortion, but don't you dare chase a fox.

Alive and Well

When I think back to my first hunt, the pleasant impression it made still lingers: images of gentlemen in scarlet coats on horseback as one would only expect to see galloping past thatched roofs in the countryside of England. They are refreshing scenes in a world so little appreciative of ceremony, manners, and etiquette. It is comforting to know that it is not a thing of the past here in America, but even more reassuring to see that Americans are defending such values here and abroad.

While attending that hunt, I made a quick call to my mother. After I had told her I was watching a foxhunt in Pennsylvania, there was a brief silence. "Where did you say you are?" she asked. "I thought they had those only in England."

"No, Mother," I said, "not anymore. They are alive and well in America."

CHAPTER 46

Reflections on Christmases Past and Future

BY JOHN HORVAT II

When men dream, it will eventually lead to sublime things that capture the imagination and elevate the soul to God. There is no greater sublime consideration than God made Man. That is why Christmas has such an enormous attraction and inspires great dreams. Not only did God become man, but He made Himself accessible to us as the Divine Infant in Bethlehem. During Christmas, we are invited to celebrate this sublime event that is the core of all things Christian.

It is Christmas, and we all think back on Christmases past not without a bit of nostalgia for what the feast represents. We think back on Christmas trees, manger scenes, and midnight Masses. We recall family dinners, marveling children, and Christmas carols. Such memories fill us with joys in a brutal world that is ever more joyless.

The celebration of Christmas is part of our long Christian tradition. It is not only the personal memories that so capture the imagination, but our participation in this long tradition that spans centuries. We all are part, not only of our own celebrations, but we also share in celebrations in all places and all times that have welcomed the Christ Child. Whether in magnificent cathedrals or humble chapels, in good times or bad, in full freedom or in prisons, all these Christmases truly become ours, and we rightly savor them.

This is the great beauty of true tradition. Through it, we can participate in those good things of the past—and provide them a future. True tradition preserves and passes down the essence of what is most good and valuable. It preserves that which we experience and want to savor. It allows us to share joyfully with others in our families, communities, and nation a common practice that celebrates our identity and makes us who we are.

There are those who do not understand tradition. They associate it with stagnation, abuses, and restraint. They do not realize that true tradition is an affirmation and projection of one's personality and family over time. They do not see that tradition is only tradition when it is good, dynamic, and progressing. Tradition must always be purifying and perfecting itself, much like the distillation process makes excellent spirits ever freer of impurities and sediment. Tradition's memories must age over time, allowing the full flavor to appear. Thus, tradition does not distort, but rather leaves us with the pure essence of reality, from which we can progress yet more.

This is especially true of Christmas. In this case, the reality is so overwhelmingly magnificent that it is hard not to be overawed with wonder and delight. On that ineffable night when our Savior was born to Mary Ever Virgin, an immense impossibility became possible: the God-man was born. The path to our redemption was opened. It made possible a Christian order in which the Commandments and counsels were practiced.

Thus, the celebration of Christmas Eve is impregnated with the notion of the birth of Our Savior where, in that holy and silent night, one can sense the irresistible sweetness and perfection that emanates from the Divine Infant in the manger in Bethlehem. Christmas thus calls and invites us to celebrate and observe our holy traditions.

We are called to do this in a neo-pagan and commercialized world that tries to take Christ out of Christmas. Yet, the power of Christ is ironically highlighted, not diminished, by these efforts. Despite all the forces that conspire against Him, the celebration of the birth of this tiny Child stops Wall Street trading, defies communist dictators, and illuminates ugly modern buildings. This same Child also lightens the heavy hearts of those under trial, and delights the innocence of little children everywhere. The Divine Infant forces us all to put aside the frenetic intemperance of our days and turn for a moment toward that which is most important: the adoration of our God.

Our Christmas traditions still survive because we rightly hold on to the distillation of memories made sublime over the ages. Let us make this our defense against the empty din of soulless holiday spending and parties. Our joyful celebrations must vanquish the secular retailers who wage their shameless war on a merry Christmas. Our public displays must welcome the Christ Child who is banished from the public square.

If we do this, our efforts will make future Christmas memories yet more sublime, for in saner times to come, it will be recalled that when Christ was abandoned by a postmodern world, there were those who remained faithful to God and upheld their traditions. There were those sublime Christians who defied the world and joined with Christians from all times and all places, joyfully proclaiming: *Puer natus est nobis, et filius datus est nobis.* "For a child is born to us, and a son is given to us." (Is. 9:6)

How Material Things Can Lead Us to God

BY JOHN HORVAT II

Sublime considerations are often provoked by material things that lift our minds to God. Many people mistakenly think there is a contradiction between the material and spiritual. Quite the contrary: God put material things here on earth so that when they are excellent, they might incite in us a desire for the greatest excellence found in God. The good, the true, and the beautiful are staircases to heaven and God.

A lady recently wrote me with a question about the role of material things in life. She was confounded by apparent contradictions between living a pious life while enjoying material things that are all around us.

She had read the stories of the saints and how they often scorned material things. Since we are all called to be saints, she reasoned, then eventually we must all adopt a life detached from the world like that of monks, nuns, or priests. However, this is difficult to do because people derive joy from eating, buying things, or enjoying beautiful music, for example, all of which are normal activities for those living in society.

The dilemma is compounded by the fact that the legitimate joys and desires of material things are not sinful in themselves, yet seem to be harmful. Thus, many find themselves vacillating between the two extremes of "secular" and religious desires. The enjoyment of material things gives rise to guilt and blame. People are even encouraged to live a frugal and austere life surrounded by misery and ugliness as a means to become holy.

Battle Between Material and Spiritual

The battle between material and spiritual, temporal and religious, has always triggered debate in the Church. On her part, the Church has always responded with balance and common sense. If some saints scorned material things, it was because they represented something good that could be given up, not something evil that must always be rejected.

The fundamental assumption of the question I was asked is that somehow the material universe is in contradiction with the spiritual world and, therefore, bad. Such was the position of the ancient Gnostics, who viewed all matter as evil.

However, the question of the lady does not plumb those depths of the debate. She does not want to go into complex dialectics of spirit and matter. She only desires to know if she might enjoy food, music, or any other material pleasure that she finds in her path. She wants to know if these are necessarily obstacles to sanctification.

The Nature of Material Goods

Material goods are hardly obstacles. God created the material universe for our good. He would not be a just God if creation were a constant temptation for our salvation. Thus, the first thing to be established is that there is no inherent contradiction between the spiritual world and material life. In fact, the enjoyment of material things is not only good, but can even be helpful toward reaching sanctification.

Obviously, our fallen nature is such that we can abuse material things and develop exaggerated attachments to them. However, this can also happen to spiritual things. The balanced position is the practice of the virtue of temperance, whereby man governs his natural appetites and passions in accordance with the norms prescribed by reason and faith.[1] When we use things with temperance, they help us become holy.

Creation Reflects the Creator

That is why created things are important. Creation speaks to us of the Creator. Since we cannot see God, we can only gain an idea of what God is like by analogy of what we see. We have a better idea of God's grandeur, for example, by coming to know the majesty of the sea. We can have a glimpse of God's might by coming to know a strong, grand oak tree. God's infinite immensity is reflected in the vast firmament of the heaven at night.

The basis of such an affirmation can be found in Saint Thomas's fourth way of proving the existence of God, whereby we come to know

---

1. Cf. *The Catholic Encyclopedia* (1912), s.v. "temperance."

God by His traits in creation.[2] This way asserts that God created a whole universe to reflect Himself, since no one creature could sufficiently mirror Him. Each creature reflects something of the goodness, truth, and beauty that God is. When we contemplate this finite work of creation, we grasp better God's infinite perfection and experience the great spiritual joy of understanding the order and meaning of things. (*Summa Contra Gentiles*, II, 45; *Summa Theologica*, I, q. 47, a. 2)

That is to say, by seeking the excellence of material things, we can better come to know and love God. We better understand ourselves and the meaning of life.

The Teaching of Saint Bonaventure

The teaching of Saint Thomas is echoed by that of his medieval contemporary, Saint Bonaventure, the Franciscan theological giant. In his great work, *The Mind's Road to God*, the saint goes one step further by calling the world "a ladder for ascending to God" where we find "certain traces (of His hand)" and we are thus "led into the way of God." In this case, material things are not just helpful aids, but necessary steps that can take us to God.

The saint claims that "all creatures of this sensible world lead the mind of the one contemplating and attaining wisdom to the eternal God." He continues, "The invisible things of God are clearly seen, from the creation of the world, being understood by the things that are made; so that those who are unwilling to give heed to them and to know God in them all, to bless him and to love him are inexcusable."

Temporal goods are means, not obstacles to sanctification. The saint claims they can be like wings that help us take flight to heavenly considerations.

Choosing the Right Things to Sanctify Oneself

Thus temporal goods are not the problem. It is our attitude toward them that is important. We must look upon temporal goods according to their nature. Thus, we are called to love those things most like unto God. We are called to seek after excellence and proportion in things because these qualities will direct us to God. At the same time, it is

---

2. Cf. Gregory Watson, "Proving the Existence of God: Argument 4," May 22, 2013, accessed Jun. 7, 2017, https://www.serviamministries.com/blog/proving-the-existence-of-god-argument-4/.

logical that we must reject those ugly and disproportional things that speak to us of disorder and sin. We must also never be satisfied with mediocre things that turn our minds away from God.

These criteria for what to seek are well expressed by the words of Saint Paul in Holy Scriptures that call upon us to look to high ideals when he says, "Finally, brothers, whatever is true, whatever is honorable, whatever is just, whatever is pure, whatever is lovely, whatever is gracious, if there is any excellence and if there is anything worthy of praise, think about these things." (Phil. 4:8)

Splendor of Christian Civilization

That is not to say that we must own all the things of excellence that we admire. Nor can we be attached to these things as an end rather than a means. Rather, it is to have a soul turned toward the excellence these things represent. It calls upon us to appreciate the beauty, excellence, and good that God puts in our path so that we might know and love Him better. It asks us to employ these criteria so that when we make or do something beautiful, we help ourselves and others to reflect God better.

That is why Christian civilization has always striven to instill splendor and beauty into the ordinary lives of men.[3] The arts and crafts flourished in Christendom. Whether it be cuisine, music, liturgy, or architecture, they all developed and moved toward perfection under the guiding hand of the Church. The culture belonged to everyone, united as they were in the quest to know God. All these marvelous things were accessible to everyone, however humble, since all could appreciate them and make them in some way a part of their quest for God.

The problem with modern civilization is that things have no meaning or common purpose in society outside of personal gratification. There is no final end that we seek to know. Thus, things are no longer means toward God, but selfish ends. Moreover, our fallen nature tends to make us distort excellence and create a civilization that moves us away from the good, true, and beautiful. It creates a civilization that exalts the false, sinful, and ugly.

Answering the Question

---

3. Plinio Corrêa de Oliveira, "What Is Christian Civilization?" Jul. 5, 2013, accessed Jun. 7, 2017, http://www.tfp.org/what-is-christian-civilization/.

Thus, we find the answer to the question. Yes, one can and should enjoy and delight in material things (even cuisine) since they are not obstacles that keep us away from God unless we make them so. They can become essential means towards our sanctification. Enjoyed with temperance, material things exist for us to know and love God more, and we err if we fail to do so.

As Saint Bonaventure says, "He who is not illumined by such great splendor of created things is blind; he who is not awakened by such great clamor is deaf; he who does not praise God because of all these effects is dumb; he who does not note the First Principle from such great signs is foolish. Open your eyes, therefore, prick up your spiritual ears, open your lips, and apply your heart, that you may see your God in all creatures, may hear Him, praise Him, love and adore Him, magnify and honor Him, lest the whole world rise against you."

W e have sought to demonstrate through these stories that the theoretical principles found in the book, *Return to Order*, can be applied to our society. In this way, the book can become more relevant to readers, who then see that these principles are found everywhere.

The "*Return to Order* moments" collected here are far from complete. Many important principles are left unillustrated by stories. Our intention in writing this book was not to provide stories for every single chapter. Rather, we have sought to supply a sampling that would inspire others with the desire to initiate their own searches for special *Return to Order* moments. We wanted to teach people how to relish these moments as a means for developing a passion for a grand return to order.

There are three conclusions that we hope readers will take from this book.

They are Everywhere

The first conclusion is that *Return to Order* moments can be found everywhere. We do not have to be scholars or specialists to find them. Because of their organic nature, they can happen anywhere we find people. Thus, they take place in airports, supermarkets, and shops. We can find them in newspapers and articles that tell these stories and spark a flash of understanding, whereby we see *Return to Order* principles play out in a special way. They can be negative or positive examples. Others are found in the inspiring stories of heroes and representative characters around us that set the tone in society.

These tales vividly tell our story, both good and bad. They are also unexpected since they cannot be planned or programmed. Sometimes, these moments come not only unexpectedly, but when least expected. They can occur when doing something quite ordinary. Other times we are the unintended witnesses of extraordinary things. These occasions are especially helped by graces that Providence often provides, so that we might advance spiritually and socially toward virtue.

However, these ubiquitous moments do take time and effort. We must look for and reflect on them. By telling our stories, we hope readers will know what to look for and to value efforts to find their own stories and reflect upon them.

Not Alone

A second conclusion is that we are not alone in perceiving these moments that the modern world does not value. These stories should encourage readers to join with others to look for stories and savor them. Often the *Return to Order* moment opens our eyes to the existence of problems that we had not perceived. When we observe them and tell others about them through stories, it makes it easier to fight against these ills.

Other *Return to Order* moments provide insight into the glories and beauty of Christian civilization. They give us attractive examples that we can use to convince others about where we need to go. The stories of great deeds, organic solutions, and sublime attitudes inspire us to see these things as sketches of an America that might yet be.

When we share these stories, we will see we are not alone in our quest for a return to order. All too often, the media and Hollywood give the idea that everyone thinks according to a liberal mindset. These stories are hidden from the general public. Those who dare to challenge this politically correct outlook are led to believe they are the only ones who think this way. By finding examples of others who dare to notice things outside this box, we can break the isolation and come to see that there are important currents in public opinion that see things as we do.

It Can Be Done

Return to Order moments prove just how false liberal ideas are and how they can be opposed. Take the example of those upholding the value of virginity in today's hypersexualized society. Such attitudes break the liberal consensus that holds that virginity cannot be practiced, especially in college. Likewise, vibrant examples can inspire actions to topple all the other idols of the modern world that undermine Christian values.

Return to Order moments demonstrate that a return to order is possible. It can be done because it is already being done. The prospect of such a return is something that is attractive to Americans. They already have yearnings and desires for an order that they sensed once existed and might yet return.

A Great Effort

Seeking out *Return to Order* moments is important. It is not a quixotic quest that has no future. The only way to turn America back to God is to a return to order.

Our proposal is simple and straightforward. The best expression of this order is found in that same order that gave rise to the West. This organic Christian society is a return to our distant roots. It is where we came from. It is a society that historically existed in Christendom. It involves returning, not to a historical past, but to a core of ordering principles that brought us so many of the institutions that are now fading: the rule of law, representative government, traditional family, and subsidiarity.

What we have sought to do is to strengthen the conviction that America will return to order by telling stories like those in this book. Returning to order will not be easy. It will take great effort. We will often face ridicule and rejection. Holding contrary opinions can involve much suffering, but that is what it will take to return to order.

By coming to know the remnants of this order that once existed and still exists today, we start a process of hope. Like embers that can be turned into a roaring fire, so also these remnants can awaken in souls great longings for the Father's house.

Indeed, the image of the Prodigal Son is fitting for our days, for modern man is like this son who took his inheritance and spent it on parties and the frenetically intemperate activities of the great city. Only when his inheritance was spent, did the son long for his Father's house.

This book was written to awaken memories of the Father's house inside souls now longing for a return. Let us return to our Father's house. It can be done.

Join America's Return to Order

This book is part of a national campaign to help America Return to Order.

Our goal is to prepare readers to avoid the economic collapse by spreading the vision and the timeless principles of an organic Christian society, which is the serene and secure pathway to restore America.

You are personally invited to join this mission.

- Get a free copy of the book, *Return to Order: From a Frenzied Economy to an Organic Christian Society—Where We've Been, How We Got Here, and Where We Need to Go* by visiting the book website at www.ReturnToOrder.org.

- Please subscribe to the *Return to Order* weekly e-newsletter at www.ReturnToOrder.org

- Then, please consider organizing a *Return to Order* study group in your church and distributing copies of the book *Return to Order* among your friends.

- If you would like to sponsor the author to speak in your community, or to inquire about more ways to support the *Return to Order* campaign, call (855) 861-8420.

- You can also follow the campaign on Facebook, Twitter, and LinkedIn.

Facebook: www.facebook.com/ReturnToOrder.org
Twitter: www.twitter.com/ReturntoOrder
LinkedIn: www.linkedin.com/in/john-horvat-23929558

For more information, contact:
Return to Order
P.O. Box 1337, Hanover, PA 17331
(855) 861-8420
jh1908@aol.com
www.ReturnToOrder.org